GODBREATHED

GODBREATHED

What It *Really* Means for the
Bible to Be Divinely Inspired

ZACK HUNT

Herald
PRESS

Harrisonburg, Virginia

Herald Press
PO Box 866, Harrisonburg, Virginia 22803
www.HeraldPress.com

Library of Congress Cataloging-in-Publication Data
Names: Hunt, Zack, author.
Title: Godbreathed : what it really means for the Bible to be divinely
  inspired / Zack Hunt.
Description: Harrisonburg, Virginia : Herald Press, [2023] | Includes
  bibliographical references.
Identifiers: LCCN 2022057918 (print) | LCCN 2022057919 (ebook) | ISBN
  9781513811833 (paperback) | ISBN 9781513811840 (hardcover) | ISBN
  9781513811857 (ebook)
Subjects: LCSH: Bible--Inspiration. | Christian life--Biblical teaching. |
  BISAC: RELIGION / Biblical Studies / Exegesis & Hermeneutics | RELIGION
  / Christian Living / Social Issues
Classification: LCC BS480 .H876 2023 (print) | LCC BS480 (ebook) | DDC
  220.1/3--dc23/eng/20230206
LC record available at https://lccn.loc.gov/2022057918
LC ebook record available at https://lccn.loc.gov/2022057919

Study guides are available for many Herald Press titles at www.HeraldPress.com.

GODBREATHED
© 2023 Herald Press, Harrisonburg, Virginia 22803. 800-245-7894.
  All rights reserved.
Library of Congress Control Number: 2022057918
International Standard Book Number: 978-1-5138-1183-3 (paperback);
  978-1-5138-1184-0 (hardcover); 978-1-5138-1185-7 (ebook)
Printed in United States of America

27 26 25 24 23   10 9 8 7 6 5 4 3 2 1

"What a winsome, accessible, and wise invitation to an evolving view of Scripture. Zack Hunt is a good guide for everyone who wants to love the Bible while knowing that taking it seriously doesn't always mean taking it literally."

SARAH BESSEY, *New York Times* bestselling author of *A Rhythm of Prayer* and *Jesus Feminist*

"Zack Hunt has written a quite refreshing book on biblical authority that is at the same time wise and passionate. He knows well the recurring pitfalls of biblical absolutism and inerrancy that yield only idolatry. And he knows the struggle to accommodate the reality of Scripture to our best learning. Along with such an incisive review of our past work on biblical authority, Hunt aims—via his Pentecostally-tinged tradition—at a view and practice of Scripture as a Spirit-propelled text that overrides our intellectual scruples and our fearful deference. The result is a book that gives life according to the relentless generosity of the Spirit of God. Readers, especially those who live with simple ideas of authority, will find the book a welcome invitation to both faith and learning."

WALTER BRUEGGEMANN, William Marcellus McPheeters Professor Emeritus of Old Testament at Columbia Theological Seminary

"It's important to recognize that inerrancy has a history and a context, just like the Bible. And Zack Hunt does this work. I gladly recommend that folks read *Godbreathed*, especially if the way they were taught to read the Bible just won't hold up any longer and they want to understand why."

JARED BYAS, author of *Love Matters More* and cohost of *The Bible for Normal People*

"When parents ask me how to read the Bible to kids in a nontoxic way, I encourage them to let their children guide the conversation. Ask your kids, 'What do you think?'—not 'What do you think I want to say?' but truly, 'What do you think?' Thanks to Zack Hunt for showing us how each of us, including our kids, are Godbreathed, and how even the smallest ones of us are worthy to authentically engage with the Bible without doctrinal boundaries."

CINDY WANG BRANDT, author of *Parenting Forward* and *You Are Revolutionary*

"While Zack Hunt and I differ on a few matters of biblical interpretation, let me be clear: *Godbreathed* is a breathtaking book about the Book. Integrating personal experience with rigorous scholarship, Zack invites readers to embrace the Bible that God gave us—in all its complexity. *Godbreathed* is a God-honoring, truth-telling, and life-giving exploration of the Bible and how we engage with it (and yes, I chose hyphenated words because Zack hates them—as you will read in his introduction). Want to know where the Bible came from, how it's been used and abused, and what role it can play in our lives today? Read *Godbreathed*. I highly recommend it!"

KURT WILLEMS, lead pastor at Brentview Church in Calgary, Alberta, and author of *Echoing Hope: How the Humanity of Jesus Redeems Our Pain*

"This book will be a drink of cool water for Christians who have wondered whether the Bible is even worth reading anymore, reintroducing them to the book through fresh eyes. It offers readers much-needed permission to rethink deeply held beliefs, providing helpful overview of the history of how we got the Bible and the role it has held in the faith since the earliest days of the church. Readers will discover a sense of delight in the Bible and the invitation it offers to a God—and a faith—worth holding on to."

GRACE JI-SUN KIM, professor of theology at Earlham School of Religion and author of *Invisible* and *Spirit Life*

"Too often we've brought to the Bible a view of God and expectations that don't fit the text. The result fails to do justice to Scripture or to a God of love. Zack Hunt argues that the problems we find in the biblical text are not obstacles but opportunities—occasions to understand God and the role of Scripture better. I recommend this readable book to those with questions about the Bible!"

THOMAS JAY OORD, theologian, philosopher, and author of *Open and Relational Theology*

"This book is at once convicting, liberating, profound, and accessible. It is about elevating the truth of the Bible in adoration of God's mystery rather than cheapening it by worshiping the words in dogmatic certainty. You cannot read *Godbreathed* and remain unchanged."

TIFFANY YECKE BROOKS, author of *Gaslighted by God: Reconstructing a Disillusioned Faith*

To Ainsley and Eleanor,
I am so incredibly grateful and proud to be your dad

TABLE OF CONTENTS

FOREWORD

When I was a kid, one of the pastors at my church started every single children's church sermon standing behind a pulpit, holding his Bible up in the air with one hand.

"Hey, boys and girls, who brought their swords with them this morning?" he would ask.

That's what this pastor called the Bible—*his sword*.

"Let's see your swords!" he'd shout, which was our cue to hold up our Bibles as high as we could.

As a roomful of kids lifted their Bibles over their heads, the pastor would ask, "What are we holding, boys and girls?"

"The Bible," we'd say in unison.

"And what is the Bible?" he'd ask.

"God's Holy Word," we'd answer.

"And when somebody tells you that the Bible is not the Word of God, what are they doing?"

"Lying!" we'd shout.

"Amen," he'd say, and then he'd tell us to open our swords to whatever chapter and verse he was preaching on that morning.

As a kid, I believed that God wrote every single word of the Bible. Moreover, I was convinced that every single word that God wrote was perfect and true, and that God spoke Shakespearean English. When I was growing up, the pastor at my conservative Baptist church told us that the only true, unadulterated version of the Bible was the King James Version published in 1611. We didn't simply worship the Bible, we worshiped the KJV 1611 Bible—the only compilation of Scripture that was authorized by God. We loved the Bible. We pledged allegiance to the Bible. And I believed that the Bible was very much a weapon, a tangible and dangerous tool that I wielded whenever I needed to fight my enemy, whether that was Satan, demonic forces, or my US history professor at the community college I attended as a young adult. Carrying my Bible made me feel powerful, brave, safe, like I was walking around with the presence of God inside my backpack.

Looking back, I can easily become embarrassed when I consider all that I believed to be true about the Bible—and how I hurt people with it, how I limited or diminished people with it, and how prideful I felt with all that I knew about it. For years, the Bible was my idol.

One does not overcome that kind of biblical misunderstanding easily or quickly. It took a decade or more to untangle myself from the web of misinformation that I was taught as a child and wholeheartedly believed to be true about the Bible.

In my opinion, the church's greatest sin is its misuse of Scripture. The number of people who have been harmed by the weaponization of "God's Holy Word" by pastors and teachers and Christian social media influencers is mind-boggling. How many women have been victimized by the church's "sword"? How many people of color have been diminished by the church's biblical misinterpretations? How many LGBTQ+ people have been uninvited to God's story because of the church's unfortunate projections on the biblical text? I could go on and on.

This is why I believe that the book you are holding is so important and so necessary for people of faith. In *Godbreathed*, Zack Hunt succinctly and intelligently unpacks the multitude of ways that biblical literalists not only abuse the intentions and purposes of the Bible but also use it as a weapon for destruction. Moreover, Zack shines light on the path forward, offering us insights for how we should be thinking about and using the biblical texts for good.

Despite all the ways my beliefs and my theology and my personal story have evolved, I have a much greater love and respect for the Bible today than I did as a young adult. Because as a friend once told me, the Bible is far too important a book to be taken literally.

—Matthew Paul Turner
coauthor of the #1 *New York Times*
bestseller *What Is God Like?*

A WORD ABOUT WORDS

Before we begin, a word about some of the words in this book.

You may have noticed on the cover that *Godbreathed* is spelled as one word, rather than its traditional spelling with a hyphen: *God-breathed*. That spelling remains throughout the book and is an intentional choice on my part. From a purely aesthetic point of view, I find the hyphen distracting and unpleasant to look at. But there's more to my choice of spelling than that. In the original Greek, the word *theopneustos*, from which we derive *godbreathed*, has no hyphen because there were no punctuation marks in ancient Greek. That may sound trivial, but by removing the punctuation mark in god-breathed I hope to recover some of the foreignness of the original language used by Paul that is often lost in translation. In dropping the hyphen, I also want to emphasize the uniqueness of this act of inspiration as something more organic than the cold mechanics of inspiration forged in the fires of fundamentalism.

You'll also no doubt notice my occasional use of *she* when referring to God. As a rule, I try to avoid gendered pronouns for God because God has no gender. But sometimes using *God* over and over again in the same sentence just sounds clunky.

This particular choice of gendered pronoun, however, is not haphazardly chosen. There is a long tradition in the church of using *she* when referring to the Spirit. Likewise, the Bible is filled with feminine language for God, including on the lips of Jesus, who compares himself to a mother hen when lamenting over Jerusalem in Matthew's gospel.

Finally, while I typically use the term *Hebrew Bible* to refer to the Jewish canon, there are places in which I use *Old Testament* instead, not to invoke "old" as a pejorative, but rather to add emphasis to how portions of the Hebrew Bible, particularly the Law, are often seen as no longer relevant in many Christian circles.

1

STOP WORSHIPING THIS BOOK!

I can still feel the shock wave that raced across the classroom when that poor Bible slammed against that ancient chalkboard. Oh, I can hear it too. That dull, violent thud still reverberates through my imagination. But in that moment, witnessing the pages of that sacred book explode like an unholy mushroom cloud rattled my soul far more than my eardrums.

I wasn't the only one desperately trying to make sense of the scene that had just unfolded before me. I could see the same horror pulsating across the classroom in the eyes of my equally stunned classmates. As we sat there bewildered and afraid, trying to process the violence we had just witnessed, our collective silence became claustrophobic.

I had sat down at my desk only a moment before the chaos. It was the first day of *Introduction to Old Testament Theology*. My shiny new Dell Latitude laptop wasn't even open yet, and it would still be several hours before Windows 95 finished booting up. But my professor—a living saint who I had always assumed would stop and apologize to an ant if he came too close to stepping on it—had suddenly transformed into the very embodiment of evil before my eyes. With a flash I could only assume were the flames of hell rising up to empower his maleficence, he had snatched his Bible off the lectern, given it a passing, almost condescending glance, and like a bat out of hell spun around and hurled it against the chalkboard where it smashed my childlike faith to pieces before falling pathetically to the ground in a heap of ruffled pages and cracked leather.

We, a classroom full of students conditioned since birth to believe the book crumbled on the ground before us was in fact God enfleshed in paper and ink, sat there motionless, bracing ourselves for the divine wrath we were sure would soon follow. We prayed for God's holy lighting to only strike our professor, sparing the rest of us who had most certainly not signed up for the blasphemous scene in which we now found ourselves held hostage.

As he surveyed our ashen and aghast faces, our professor raised his voice and declared in a firm and unambiguous voice, "Stop worshiping this book!"

Say what now?

In the excruciating quiet that continued to fill the room you could hear the nervous rattling of our souls as we tried to process what we had just witnessed. We had no time for new instructions. We were too busy sneaking glances at one another, silently conspiring to never speak of this day ever again, while nervously waiting for the dean to march through the door at any moment and fire our professor on the spot. When the dean failed to appear, we prayed fervently that Jesus would return to rapture our innocent earthly vessels from this hellscape of blasphemy and disrespect.

Now you may find yourself just as confused reading through this scene as I was experiencing it, but for radically different reasons. If so, what you have to understand is just how revered the Bible is in the sort of conservative, sometimes fundamentalist brand of American evangelicalism I grew up in. I don't just mean the Bible as an abstract concept. I mean the literal paper, ink, and binding. "It's the word of God!" we were told. Like so many of my peers, I stood in awe of its holiness. It took me years of faithful Sunday school attendance simply to find the courage to highlight verses in my Bible because drawing in my Bible felt like scribbling on the face of God. The idea of placing anything on top of my Bible—or any other Bible for that matter—felt akin to blasphemy. This was, I believed, the very presence of God on earth. Tossing it nonchalantly on the couch or leaving it underneath a pile of junk mail felt sinful.

Even when I reached the ripe old age of middle school and finally worked up the courage to highlight verses in my Bible, the wellspring of that courage was anything but noble. I would have told you I was highlighting my favorite verses so I could find them faster and therefore be better prepared to share them "in season and out" with sinners who needed my theological tutelage. In truth, I started highlighting verses in my Bible because I saw others doing it who seemed like they loved and adored the Bible more than me and I wanted people to know I was the better Christian.

Tragically, that sanctified graffiti was the opening of the floodgates of biblical desecration. Like the juvenile delinquents whose souls I had hoped to save from hell, I quickly progressed from highlighting Bible verses to more hardcore biblical vandalism. And before you could say *Melchizedek* my beloved *WOW 1997 Student Bible* was so covered in stickers and Jesus graffiti it looked like it was one fairy godmother away from springing to life and passing out W.W.J.D. (What Would Jesus Do) bracelets at a Newsboys concert.

If you're not familiar with *WOW*, it's because you had better taste in music as a teenager than I did. *WOW* was a soundtrack collection of the year's top contemporary Christian music songs. It was modeled on, well let's be honest, completely ripped off from, the *Now That's What I Call Music* series. The *WOW* Bible was another way to milk the cash cow of faith. Excuse me, I mean extend the worship experience. I had purchased my *WOW 1997 Student Bible* with my own money, a rare accomplishment in my teenage years, and treated it like it was destined for the Smithsonian. That is, until my existential need for others to see how much I loved the Bible took over, thus beginning my fall into the sort of biblical hooliganism I would have had myself burned at the stake for just a few years earlier.

I proceeded cautiously, only a few verses highlighted here and there to test God's patience. Not being struck down by lightning was a sign I could press on. The highlighted verses were soon followed by stickers. Lots and lots of stickers. Mostly Christian band stickers so people would know that not only did I read my Bible all the time, but when I wasn't reading my Bible I was listening to the Bible put to music. I also made sure to squeeze in a few "Jesus Is My Lifeguard"–type stickers so people knew I was clever and funny and someone you would definitely want to invite to a party, even though I would never go to that party because going to parties was a sin.

But then one day tragedy struck. The spine of my *WOW* 97 Bible began to crack. At first I mourned what seemed like the loss of my greatest source of pride. Then I remembered I'm from the South, and in the South we can fix anything and everything with duct tape. So my otherwise light blue *WOW* 97 Bible became an otherwise light blue *WOW* 97 Bible with a distinctive gray duct-taped spine. I realize that may seem a bit sad to you, or perhaps like I was being a cheapskate, but in my mind it made me feel like an even better Christian than I already thought I was.

Now you might be thinking to yourself, "But if you were willing to put stickers and duct tape on your Bible, didn't that mean it had dropped a few levels of reverence in your mind?" Absolutely not. First of all, I was an evangelical teenager on fire for God. Things like logic and reason were irrelevant, if not sinful. More importantly, church camp was coming up that summer and true Christians don't go to church camp without their Bible.

The year I took my duct tape bound *WOW 97* Bible with me to church camp, one of the camp leaders happened to sit down next to me before service and noticed the condition it was in. Rather than making an unfunny youth pastor joke about my apparent inability to take care of the things I owned,[1] he remarked about how obvious it was that I loved and read my Bible by the fact that it was held together by duct tape. My face beamed with so much pride I was like Moses coming down from Sinai after communing with God. No longer was my Bible just a Bible. It was my way of showing the rest of the world I was a better Christian than they were. After all, I read my Bible so much it had to be held together by duct tape. And where was theirs? Probably sitting on a shelf somewhere collecting dust under a pile of old church bulletins they never even bothered to read.

So that first day in *Introduction to Old Testament Theology* as I stared at my professor's Bible lying helplessly on the ground and let his edict ramble through my brain, I genuinely struggled to make sense of what I had just witnessed. *What was he thinking? Didn't he know this was the word of God? Did he want to burn in hell forever?* Surely that was a stunt Bible he threw against the chalkboard, some other book he put a fake Bible cover on so his soul would not be damned for eternity. But if it wasn't a stunt Bible and he really was the kind of faithful, Jesus-loving, God-fearing, Bible-adoring Christian I thought he was up until that very moment, had I somehow not understood the Bible the way I thought I had? But how could that be when I had never missed a day of Sunday school and had a shelf full of Bible quizzing trophies at home to prove my biblical expertise? Worse, if I stayed in this class and listened to what he had to say would I turn out like my professor and find myself on the path to hell? Or worse still, would I become . . . a liberal?

Years later, when I was out on my own working as a youth pastor, long after I thought I had given up the idolatry my professor warned me about, I still found myself struggling with his prophetic act. I tried recreating it for the students in my youth group, thinking such a provocative stunt would have the same jarring and transformative effect on them that it once had on me, but I failed to be the edgy youth pastor I imagined in my dreams. The best I could do was drop it gently on the ground, and as your imagination will tell you, gently dropping a Bible on the ground isn't nearly as impactful as seeing one slammed against the wall. I was long past worrying about stacking something on top of my Bible, but biblical idolatry still had a firm hold on me.

When I say biblical idolatry I don't mean I was bowing down before the Bible in my bedroom every night before bed chanting and burning incense. That would be weird. And even though I was definitely a weird kid, I wasn't *that* weird. But I was radically, irrationally, cultishly devoted to a book. Not just its message, but its physical existence. The cardboard cover now covered in stickers. The pages drenched in highlights. The red letters. Even the glue that bound page to cover.

All of it was holier than angels' wings and even further beyond questioning than my grandmother telling me I couldn't leave the dinner table until I tried at least one bite of the new recipe she made for Sunday dinner.

Look, I get it. Idolatry is not a word or concept that has much resonance to the modern ear, but it's something all of us practice at one point or another in one way or another. That's because idolatry isn't about little golden statues hidden in the jungle awaiting the arrival of Indiana Jones. In the context of the Christian faith, idolatry is a matter of life and death. Not because capital punishment is involved, but because idolatry is about where we turn or who we turn to or what we rely on to make it through life.

If we believe God is the source of all life, then unquestioned, misguided, unhealthy devotion to anything else is deadly. Not because it kills the body—though it could—but because it destroys the soul. Idolatry is about the things we devote our lives to that aren't God, and there are many options for that in life. Whether it is work, money, fame, or some other obsession, if it becomes the center of our life, disordering and disrupting our relationships, bleeding our souls dry of joy and denying us the abundant life we've been created for, then we have likely fallen into idolatry because we've cut ourselves off from the real source of hope and joy and life itself.

So how can letting the Bible lead your life be idolatry? Therein lies the problem. Behind a question like that is a subtle but problematic assumption that the Bible and God are interchangeable, that they are one and the same; to say one is to say both. But the Bible, as divinely inspired as it might be, is not God. It's a book. Or rather a collection of books. But it is not the Word, the Logos of God, the Word made flesh. The Bible is very clear that honor belongs to Jesus (John 1:1–4).

But when we treat the Bible and God as interchangeable
something else happens, often without us even realizing it.
Because the Bible doesn't exist on its own, and because it was
written by people in a culture and time far removed from our
own, it requires interpretation. So when we make God and the
Bible interchangeable, what we are also doing—albeit unintentionally—is making ourselves, or rather our interpretation
of the Bible, interchangeable with God. In seeking to better
worship our Creator, we too often put ourselves in the place
of the Creator as the source of all knowledge, of truth and
life, sanctification and damnation. There may be whispers of
truth in the message we proclaim, but inevitably and unavoid-
ably when God and the Bible become interchangeable, it is
our truth, or rather our version of the truth, that becomes the
gospel. And so without ever realizing it, the God we end up
worshiping, while perhaps bearing some resemblance to the
God described in the Bible, is ultimately the creation of the
one staring at us in the mirror. Biblical idolatry is not just
about worshiping a book, it's about worshiping ourselves.

When this happens, the Bible ceases to be a living document
full of life-giving good news, and instead becomes calcified
behind the walls of our limited understanding and personal
biases, frozen in the rigor mortis of our interpretation, and
transformed into a weapon of death to wield against our enemies. In our hands, the book of life becomes a book of death.

Whether we intend to or not, we inevitably follow our own
ideas about what is right. That is what it means to practice
personal judgment. The problem arises when we deny the role
our own judgment plays in developing our faith, sanctifying
our ideas as the unfiltered word of God, and forcing others to
live the sorts of lives we believe they should. Or as we like to
tell ourselves, we believe the Bible says they should.

Ironically, this is exactly what the Bible itself warns us about when it teaches that idolatry leads to death. We tend to think about idolatry leading to death in purely physical or literal terms, in the sense that there are Old Testament laws against worshiping other gods, such as the first of the Ten Commandments. Worship one of those gods and you might be stoned to death. But death from idolatry doesn't always work that way. Deuteronomy 17 does require stoning to death for those found guilty of worshiping other gods, but most of the prohibitions against idol worship in the Old Testament don't come with that particular punishment. In Deuteronomy 4, for example, the death and destruction God warns of is being cast out from the nomadic camp the people of Israel called home and scattered into the wilderness alone. Being lost and alone in the wilderness could certainly lead to death by virtue of no longer being connected to the source of life. However, as we continue to read the story of the people of God as it unfolds in the Hebrew Bible we find that neither penalty seems to have done much to curtail the people's idolatry.

If we pay careful attention to the words of the prophets,[2] we'll notice the people of God were almost always worshiping other gods alongside Yahweh and yet few if any of them—outside the prophets of Baal, who had the audacity to go toe to toe with Elijah—faced the death penalty for their idolatry (1 Kings 18:40).

The sort of death that comes through idolatry is more often a spiritual death that inevitably and inescapably comes about when we cut ourselves off from the Spirit, the source of life—when we replace God with something or someone else as the source of our devotion. Idolatry leads to death because without the breath of God in our lungs, we cannot breathe. Without that sacred breath, death inevitably finds us all. When this inversion of the created order happens, when we make ourselves gods of our own lives but without the ability to breathe out new life, the spiritual death inside us begins to seep out, infecting others with the sort of spiritual death and damnation we heap on those we deem undeserving of the love and grace we have been gifted.

When we transform the Bible into the divine, or more accurately our interpretation of the Bible into "a biblical worldview," we begin to focus on the story we *think* it tells, rather than the story we are being invited into. When we conclude we have the Bible figured out, we end up telling others where they belong instead of trying to figure out our own place within the story of the people of God. We begin to tell a new story of our own creation and we have become very bad storytellers. We tell stories about exclusion and damnation, oppression and misogyny, of condemnation of the poor and scapegoating the stranger, and we do it all in the name of God.

When we put bad stories in the mouth of God, we smother what the Hebrew Bible calls the *ruach* of God, the very breath of God—that is to say, the Spirit herself from blowing how and where she will and to and through whom she will. This sort of idolatry kills, sometimes physically, but always spiritually. It should come as no surprise then to see the Bible lose not just its place of authority in modern life, but also its relevance or appeal to anyone not already warming a pew on Sunday morning. After all, who would want to be part of a story that crushes your spirit with constant judgment and damnation?

We have to learn to tell a better story—even if it doesn't result in a single new person joining our membership rolls. That is, after all, what the Bible is calling us to do: continue telling the story of the people of God. Not just by memorizing and quoting Bible verses, but by living out that story ourselves in and for the world around us.

That invitation isn't an easy one. In fact, it's often quite painful learning that the thing you thought you knew so well you didn't really know at all. But passing through the refining fires of intellectual honesty and historical reality is an essential crucible for faith. We can't claim to be a people of the truth if we're devoted to bearing false witness for the sake of maintaining our dogmatic beliefs. Admitting we could be wrong about the things we are most convinced of, that are so fundamental to who we are, is painful and scary, because embarrassment is painful and becoming someone new is scary.

But fear not. While refinement can be painful, those tongues of fire are the Spirit of God, and the Spirit brings life. The refining of the Spirit is a necessary and purifying, and ultimately liberating, fire that prepares us for the complex, challenging, and sometimes embarrassing reality of the story of God's people. It is only from there that the scales of presupposition and dogma can begin to fall from our eyes so that we may begin to see the good news where it is, and just as importantly where it is not. It is from this biblical rebirth that we can begin to reimagine divine inspiration not as a form of heavenly dictation, but a Spirit-infused, wholly saturated way of life that begets more life. This is the indwelling of the Spirit in our lives, this inspiration, literally the in-Spirit-ing of our very being. Or as the Bible calls it, being godbreathed (2 Timothy 3:16).

Godbreathed things live and grow. They don't sit on a shelf collecting dust like that book that's sitting on your shelf right now that you swore you were going to read on the beach last summer. (You know the one.) For that growth to happen, we need to make space for the Spirit to live and move and have her way in our lives. The Holy Spirit doesn't force her way into our lives. She stands waiting to be invited in. We need to make space and allow the Spirit to move in and among us, teaching us the story of the good news, but also helping us imagine new ways the good news can be understood and applied in the ever-evolving contexts of history and culture. That doesn't mean making the Bible more palatable for the prevailing culture. It means telling the same story we've been telling for two thousand years. But telling it in new and fresh ways that take into account everything we've learned over those two thousand years in order to tell our story in ways that make sense to our neighbors, that relate to their lives, that are intellectually honest, and most importantly, that are truly good news.

There are those who see any deviation from reading and understanding the Bible in the way they believe it has always been read and understood as a low view of Scripture that doesn't take it seriously. But asking hard questions about the Bible and refusing to settle for worn-out answers is not a low view of Scripture. Nor is making something relatable and practical the same as making something comfortable. Making space for the Spirit to open our eyes and transform our minds, remaking us anew each and every day, is a deeply serious and sometimes painfully honest approach to the story of our faith. More importantly, making space for the Spirit holds the Bible in a place of true reverence, giving thanks to God for the gift that has been given and the invitation that has been extended to us to join in the transformative storytelling of God's people. This sort of Spirit-led positioning resists the biblical idolatry that has for so long plagued the church, because the Bible in this dynamic no longer exists as something to exploit for our purposes. Instead it is transformed into a journey we are invited to join, learn from, and mourn over when we get it wrong. Most importantly, setting the Spirit free to guide our reading of Scripture allows the Bible to be truly good news on earth as it is in heaven.

This isn't a new approach to Scripture. In fact, it's an incredibly ancient one. This sort of understanding of divine inspiration was first articulated by the earliest church fathers. And the honest wrestling and questioning of Scripture I'm suggesting? Not only is wrestling with God a practice found all throughout the Bible, but our Jewish brothers and sisters have been doing the very same for countless generations in yeshivas, where they are trained to ask questions and challenged to partner with God to develop new understandings of God's word for our ever-changing times and new contexts.

For centuries, our Christian forebears unapologetically wrestled with Scripture as well, asking hard questions of the text and delving deep to uncover the mysteries that lay beyond the literal words on the page—that is, at least until the idea of biblical inerrancy was invented in the late nineteenth century, and questioning or criticizing Scripture became a sin in fundamentalist circles.

That's not to say fundamentalists who believe in biblical inerrancy don't also evoke the language of wrestling with Scripture, but the form of wrestling with Scripture often embraced in fundamentalism is more akin to professional wrestling. Within the rigid ideological framework of fundamentalism, a reader can go through the motions of wrestling with the meaning of Scripture, but that meaning was decided long before the match ever began. Which makes a certain kind of sense, at least in that world. When right beliefs are the key to salvation, there is no room for doubt or questioning or honest exploration that sets the Spirit free to guide us where she will. All that matters is getting the answer right. And when salvation becomes a zero-sum game, we inevitably end up loving ideas more than people, particularly when those people's ideas about faith, God, and the Bible are different from our own.

When that happens—when being right is more important than loving our neighbor—we shouldn't be surprised to see people emptying the pews in droves and the church's reputation in tatters. What good news is there in a cold and lifeless answer book? Who wants to be part of a story that seems to only condemn and exclude and has little if any effect on life in the here and now? If we really love our neighbor the way we profess to love them, then shouldn't we be desperately seeking a better story to tell than the one we've been telling them? One that is overflowing with life-changing good news instead of fear-mongering and threats of damnation?

We need a more audacious faith, one that trusts the Spirit to guide us where she may. The sort of faith that isn't afraid of asking questions or knocking on doors of inquiry that have long been locked shut. We need the sort of faithful courage it takes to allow the Spirit to lead wherever she may take us as we openly, honestly, and unapologetically read and examine the text. We need to draw from our past, our present, and even from our brothers and sisters in other traditions in order to rebuild a healthier relationship with Scripture, and by extension, God and neighbor.

We need a better understanding of what the Bible is, what the Bible is not, where it comes from, and how it is inspired in order for it to play the sort of life-giving and liberating role it was always intended to play in our lives. That role and whether the Bible becomes a source of life and liberation, or is used to oppress, marginalize, or even sanctify the killing of our enemies, isn't a responsibility we can push off onto the text. It's up to us.

We can't excuse away our prejudices, bigotry, misogyny, and racism with Bible verses. We must take ownership of the ways we have weaponized and abused Scripture for our own ends, repent, and rebuild a new, healthier relationship with the word of God. We must stop using the Bible to sanctify our opinions as the word of God.

We must learn to tell a good story, a life-giving story, a story worth believing in. And that won't happen until we come to terms with what the Bible really is and what it is not. As another former professor of mine once wrote, "One of the most persistent themes of the Hebrew Bible is the critique of idolatry. This applies not only to carved or molten statues, but to the human tendency to absolutize things that are merely part of the created order. Perhaps the greatest irony in the history of the Bible is that it itself has so often been treated as an idol and venerated with a reverential attitude while its message is ignored. Biblical figures from Abraham to Job do not hesitate to argue with the Almighty. The least that might be expected of readers of the Bible is that they bring the same critical spirit to bear on the biblical text."[3]

RICHARD KILEY
WROTE THE BIBLE

When I was a child I spoke like a child, I understood like a child, I played sick to stay home from school like a child—and I don't mean to brag, but I would like to think I had something of a gift for it. Maybe you did too. If you were also a gifted child actor, perhaps you also found yourself at your grandparents' house for the day while your parents worked and all those other suckers went to school. If you did find yourself in such a situation, I have no doubt you also have vivid memories of watching *The Price Is Right*. It was a rite of passage in childhood, at least in the prehistoric pre-Netflix days of the earlier nineties. To this day, playing just one game of Plinko remains high on my bucket list, even if *The Price Is Right* no longer signals a day of freedom and relaxation.

As you know well, *The Price Is Right* doesn't last all day. So I had to find other ways to fill my time at home "sick." But that was okay because I had cutting edge historical entertainment at my fingertips—a trail to blaze, a family to raise, and a new home to reach in Oregon. Or I would have if I wasn't constantly dying of dysentery or drowning my team of oxen in the river. When my *Oregon Trail* family did die, a regrettably frequent occurrence, I was off to find where in the world Carmen Sandiego had escaped to, though I'm ashamed to admit she eluded my detective skills more often than not.

Eventually the thrills of watching falling Plinko chips and leading my green pixelated family across the frontier began to wane. Thankfully, it was around this time that my grand-mother decided to invest in a very special collection of VHS tapes for me and my siblings. Not as an incentive to play hooky from school. They weren't reserved for viewing on sick days. We could watch them anytime, though they weren't there to simply keep us entertained. They were spiritual nourishment. The word made cartoon and bound in black polyester plastic to keep our young minds growing in wisdom and favor and stature with God and man. Or at least keep us out of our grandmother's hair for thirty minutes at a time.

The name of that blessed cartoon series has been lost to history or at least my memory. Regardless, the premise was straightforward: famous Bible stories in cartoon form that would arrive in the mail once a month. Sort of like a Chris-tian Netflix, but less efficient. Noah, Moses, Jonah, Jesus, they were all there, and my brother and sister and I loved each and every one of them and genuinely got excited whenever a new video would arrive in the mail. Judge my conservative evan-gelical upbringing all you want, but there are only so many failed searches for Carmen Sandiego and watching your green pixelated pioneer family die on the *Oregon Trail* one kid can handle before boredom sets in and he gets desperate.

I enjoyed those biblical cartoons for far longer than I care to admit, but as I got older the excitement of cartoon Bible stories began to wane along with the integrity of the physical tapes themselves. As the static began to creep into the images from too many rewatches and I began entering my teenage years, my interest in biblically-based entertainment became more . . . I want to say sophisticated, but who am I kidding? I've always been a Bible nerd and there's no pretending otherwise now. Regardless of motivation, my grandmother was there to ease my boredom once again with new, elevated forms of biblical entertainment on VHS. Rather than cartoons, these new videos were top-notch Hollywood-caliber movies starring the *Jurassic Park* tour guide voice of Richard Kiley as the apostle Matthew retelling the gospel of Matthew. The premise was that Matthew was dictating his memoirs to a scribe who would write down everything he said, between cutaways to what I assumed were historically accurate reenactments of the events he was describing to his young squire. As a kid, this made perfect sense to me. Matthew wrote the gospel of Matthew. I mean he had to, right? His name is right there on the title page.

Obviously Matthew wasn't taking field notes while following Jesus around Galilee. How could he? His hands were full, passing out fish and loaves. But writing a memoir after the fact? That checked out. And why not have a scribe do the actual writing? Matthew was too old and too important to be distracted by manual tasks when what was really important was getting all the facts right. Which he did, of course, and in perfect order and all with verbatim quotes because as viewers like me knew, the Holy Spirit, though invisible on the screen, was present, whispering everything in Matthew's ear for the scribe to write down.

In my defense, this is more or less how many folks assume the Bible came together. It's a fair assumption. When books are written today the actual author who wrote them typically puts their name on the cover as they have for nearly as long as there have been books. And when we write history today, getting the precise historical details is of paramount importance for that history to be thought true. If all of that is bound together, we consider it a single unified book with a single unified message. We do this with the Bible too before we ever pick it up, assuming we ever do. But you know what they say happens when you assume: it creates a situation wherein holy Scripture is used in terribly misinformed ways to cause great damage both intentionally and unintentionally in the name of God.

The Bible is unlike any other text most of us will ever read and we must treat it as such if we're ever going to have any hope of understanding the story, its writers, and by extension what God is trying to tell us. That's because the Bible isn't just a book. The Bible is a complex web of storytelling, songs, history, apocalypse, chronologies, parables, laws, and opinions from a wide variety of writers with nearly as diverse time periods and cultural contexts in which they wrote. We can't simply pick up a Bible and expect to read it with the same ease of comprehension we would with *Harry Potter* or even Wikipedia because the Bible is nothing like *Harry Potter* or Wikipedia. It's a collection of documents written in particular contexts for a particular people with particular ways of understanding God and the world that are often much different than our own.

But that doesn't leave us without hope. The spiritual riches of the Bible are there to be mined by whoever would seek them. It takes effort, though, to find treasures hidden in a field. They're not just lying on top of the dirt waiting for any poor sap to stumble by, put them in their pocket, and amble away home. There's work to be done, effort to be extended, and understanding that has to be accumulated if we are to have any hope of understanding what the Bible is, where it came from, why it exists, and what its many authors are trying to tell us. If we are going to have any hope of unraveling the mysteries of this godbreathed story and whatever it might be trying to tell us about our own lives, we first have to understand where the story came from. Who wrote it. How it came together. How it's been made and remade, edited and revised, fought over and brought together by common assent. To understand the story of the people of God, we first have to tell the story of how that story came to be.

So, where did the Bible come from? And what is it really? Is it even a book, or is it possibly something else altogether? To answer those questions, we have to go back to the beginning. Not to the time of talking snakes and magical trees, but to the very beginning of the story of the Bible before the Bible was even a glimmer of an idea in anyone's mind, before a single word was written down or pen was dipped in ink. Back to the moment of genesis when the story of the people of God was told only by the spoken word. Around a campfire, while doing chores, or out in the fields the people of God told their story to one another, their children, their neighbors, or even themselves as they lay beneath the stars at night wondering how the world came to be.

Long before there was a book, there were stories. Stories about hope and liberation, about burning bushes and clouds of locusts, about a garden and a rainbow, a colorful coat, and the promise of one day going on to something better. As these stories were told and retold, they eventually found their way to the pen of a professional scribe or some other literate member of the community. The stories usually weren't their own, and they didn't always set out to write an entire book, at least not the sort of book the Gideons have tucked away in the drawers of hotel rooms around the world.

The writing of the big book would have started with smaller individual stories, songs, poems, prophecies, and laws. Some scribes even wrote different versions of the same story. Others cleaned up a story to make sure all the right details were there. Still others pasted together different accounts so as to make sure the reader didn't miss anything. Eventually these writings came together as books, sometimes with important people's names attached to them to catch the reader's attention and let them know that what they were reading had some authority behind it.[1]

Though most readers already knew there was authority behind the stories because the stories weren't new. They didn't need an orientation class to understand why they were important. They were *their* stories. The people's stories. God's story told through the lives, voices, imaginations, frustrations, failures, aches, pains, and joys of the people of God. They had lived through what gave the stories their collective importance. They had lived their truth. But when did that storytelling begin? If we take the internal timeline of the Bible at face value, the events described in the Hebrew Bible begin unfolding somewhere around the time of King Tut in the fourteenth century BCE.[2] Of course, if you're a literal six-day creationist the math gets a bit fuzzy here, and you're stuck with various world cultures existing before the world was created. Nevertheless, many scholars believe the oldest written part of the story of the people of God probably dates from somewhere around the ninth or eighth century BCE.[3] That bit of writing is thought to be Judges 5, and it's not hard to imagine why.[4]

Judges 5 records the song of Deborah. Songs are easy to remember. I can't remember anything I read in graduate school from Friedrich Schleiermacher but at the drop of a hat I can sing along with every line of "Uptown Funk." Songs are all the more easy to remember when, like Deborah's song, they tell

the story of our liberation from oppression. Throw in a line or
two about a woman named Jael driving a tent peg through the
temple of the sleeping tyrant Sisera and it begins to make sense
why this song may be the first written account in the Hebrew
Bible. It's particularly interesting that this story could be the
oldest account in Scripture given how deeply patriarchal the
books of the Bible can be. If Judges 5 is indeed the oldest written account in Scripture, then the story of the people of God
begins with taking down the patriarchy. If the Hebrew Bible
begins with a literal overthrow of patriarchy by a woman, and
the New Testament begins with a young woman being chosen
to bring into the world the One who will bring "down rulers
from their thrones"—rulers who were exclusively male—and
if that One in turn ordained women to be the first ones to
preach the good news of his resurrection to men who were
cowering in fear, it's enough to make you stop and wonder if
perhaps God isn't quite as enthusiastic about male leadership
as many men in the church would like us to believe. Or at least
it should.

Whether Judges 5 is indeed the oldest written portion of
Scripture or not, the earliest archaeological evidence we have
for events written about in the Bible comes from the ninth to
eighth century BCE, right around the same time ancient Rome
was founded.[5] What is known as the Law or the Pentateuch,
the first five books of the Hebrew Bible, was likely written
during a time of exile in the sixth century BCE.[6]

Those books were written in Hebrew, the language of the
people of Israel, but not necessarily the language of every
member of God's tribe. So sometime in the fourth century
BCE, the existing books of the Hebrew Bible were translated
into Greek in a document known as the Septuagint, a word
derived from the Latin word *septuaginta* meaning "seventy."[7]

While the Septuagint was being finished, Daniel, the last and at times one of the most mysterious books of the Hebrew Bible, was written. But once it was, the Hebrew Bible, or what Christianity has come to call the Old Testament, still wasn't quite ready to be bound, published, and shipped off for distribution.

We like to imagine the Bible came together as each new book was written, but canon formation doesn't always have a specific date we can point to and say, "This is when the canon was officially closed." Such was the case during the time of Jesus. The Judaism of his day had a more fluid list of books that comprised Hebrew Scripture than our Bibles today. There was certainly a core body of texts, such as the Pentateuch, which contained the Law, and by the end of the first century of the Common Era the Hebrew Bible had a settled canon, but during Jesus' lifetime other books made their way in and out of Jewish circles of scriptural authority, with some eventually making the final cut while others became "apocryphal."[8] That doesn't mean they were about the end times or the apocalypse. Rather, they were considered important works that contained accepted wisdom, but for various reasons did not quite rise to the level of holy Scripture. So, when Jesus talks about "all the Law and the Prophets" in the Gospels, he's not necessarily referring to the exact same list of thirty-nine books in the modern Hebrew Bible.

The books of the New Testament that record the life and teaching of Jesus also had their own interesting formation. If you grew up in the church, then perhaps like me you either were led to believe the books of the New Testament were written contemporaneously with the events they recorded or you just assumed that to be the case because nobody likes writing book reports after the fact. Either way, that was not the case. And to make things even more complicated, the New

Testament is also out of order, at least as the chronology of the actual writing goes.

The oldest written sections of the New Testament are generally accepted to be the letters of Paul,[9] though scholars do not believe every letter ascribed to Paul was actually written by him,[10] making their dating much later, probably sometime toward the end of the first century CE. The earliest of Paul's letters is, depending on whose dating you accept, either his first letter to the Thessalonians or his letter to the Galatians.[11] We're talking a difference of probably just a few years between the two, with both dating to somewhere in the middle of the first century CE, or about two decades after the death of Jesus.

The Gospels don't arrive in written form until after Paul's letters, sometime in the middle to end of the first century, with the gospel of Mark being the earliest of the four gospels.[12] That's not to say the stories weren't being circulated earlier in one form or another, either as oral tradition or possibly as shorter, written notes with what would become the Gospels. This may have been particularly the case with Mark. Mark may have been not so much designed as a single volume, but rather as a collection of notes, a sort of scrapbook of stories and sayings and parables for speakers—or evangelists—to refer to that were eventually brought together by an editor who arranged them into what we know as the gospel of Mark.[13]

What makes this process particularly interesting is that, if true, there was no original manuscript of a gospel like Mark because it wasn't composed in the same way a manuscript or book is composed today, as an intentionally thought-out and planned single work. For those who look to the original manuscript for scriptural perfection, this lack of an original manuscript, at least in the form we imagine when we use that phrase today, has some interesting implications for the belief in biblical inerrancy, which we will look at in the next chapter.

Since a significant amount of similar material in both Matthew and Luke also appears in Mark, it is believed they both drew their shared material from Mark, forming a group known by scholars as the synoptic gospels for the way they share a common view or presentation of the life and teachings of Jesus.[14] Matthew and Luke were both likely written at the end of the first or early second century.[15] John is the latest gospel, appearing sometime in the early second century with the most distinct stories and sayings that appear nowhere else in the other gospels.[16] The book of Acts is often thought of as originally having been a single volume with Luke, with the original manuscript possibly having been written on two separate scrolls due simply to constraints of space.

The rest of the New Testament epistles follow after Luke-Acts, with the always fun and wacky but sometimes blood-drenched book of Revelation bringing up the rear at the end of the first century. Though if some bishops had had their way, Revelation wouldn't have made the final cut.[17] In fact, even today there are Christian traditions such as the Orthodox Church that either do not include it in their canon or simply leave it out of their liturgy.[18]

By the end of the second century of the Common Era, all the books of what we call the New Testament had been written, and the names and total number of books listed by bishops like Irenaeus, among others. Though curiously Irenaeus believed it was the traditions preserved in the books of the New Testament that made it holy, not the books themselves.[19] Additionally, what constituted the canon of the New Testament wasn't always the exact same list of books. The oldest surviving list of New Testament books that matches our list today comes from

Athanasius in the fourth century CE.[20] However, in the first four centuries of the church, we have at least a dozen different lists of books that comprised the early New Testament, though they largely resemble the list of New Testament books we have now.[21] And right around here is where the conspiracy theories often begin, most of them deriving from a single book and later blockbuster film: *The DaVinci Code*. As entertaining as the book and movie might have been, Dan Brown's depiction of the closing of the biblical canon at the Council of Nicaea is, like the rest of his book, a work of fiction.

It is certainly true that Emperor Constantine called together the various bishops across the Roman Empire to the town of Nicaea to hold a council to unite the empire by clarifying things that needed clarifying. To that end a creed was written and a priest named Arius was condemned as the first heretic. What they did not do, however, was form a secret cabal and dictate whole cloth to the rest of the Christian world what books were and were not going to make it into the Bible. It's true, they more or less closed the canon in Nicaea, meaning they wrote down a final list of what books counted as the Bible, but the books weren't chosen or rejected based on the nefarious machinations of the bishops present in Nicaea. The bishops met to officially affirm books already in wide acceptance and use in the early church. They were in effect putting a seal of approval on something already agreed upon because the truth found in those books had been experienced in the lives of the early church.[22]

Now there were definitely many books that did not make the cut. Books like the *Gospel of Thomas*, the *Gospel of Philip*, the *Apocalypse of Paul*, and the *Sophia of Jesus* were discovered in an ancient graveyard near Nag Hammadi, Egypt, in 1945. They revolutionized our knowledge of Christian and gnostic texts written in the decades and centuries following Jesus' death. But they weren't rejected in a cover-up. Most simply weren't in as wide use or didn't line up with the accepted orthodoxy of the early church, while others weren't supported by the facts as most in the early church generally understood them, such as the aforementioned *Gospel of Philip*, which seems to claim that Jesus and Mary Magdalene were married. And some were, well, just too weird or frankly appalling, like the *Gospel of Thomas*, which claims that the child Jesus once killed another kid for bumping into him.

It's not that these books were covering up the truth. They simply weren't the truth as understood and experienced by the early church. There wasn't, despite *The DaVinci Code*'s exciting prose, a dark conspiracy to suppress the "truth" of other gospels or letters. The Council of Nicaea affirmed what was already affirmed by the community of faith. There was no book burning.

And then the canon was closed.

Well, mostly.

At least for the church based in Rome.

Unfortunately for those looking for a nice, neat, streamlined history of the Bible, Christianity wasn't exhausted by those practicing the faith on the Italian peninsula. We tend to think of early Christianity as a monolith, but that couldn't be further from the truth. It would be more accurate to think of Christianities, plural, than one single and united group of believers during the decades and even centuries after the events recorded in the Gospels.[23] From the very first days of the faith there was great diversity in both thought and practice. As Paul alludes to in his first letter to the church in Corinth (1 Corinthians 1:11–12), various leaders formed—whether intentionally or not—their own followings. This is why we have so many and various texts and would-be scriptural writings in the early days of the faith. People were still trying to figure out who this Jesus was, what his teachings meant, and how to make sense of the resurrection.

These groups coalesced over time, but even then, everything didn't flow out of Rome, or even Jerusalem. African Christianity was critical in the development of the faith. Early church fathers like Origen and Augustine, whom we will look at later, were both from Alexandria, Egypt. Syrian Christians, home of Damascus where Paul had his famous encounter with Jesus, formed their own traditions, and Ethiopian Christianity, which still flourishes today and even claims to be home to the actual Ark of the Covenant, is as old as any tradition you can find in Christianity.

So when we talk about big moments in the history of the church, it's important to remember that we often do so from the perspective of Western European or Roman Christianity. It's true that the church was certainly more unified then than it is today and remained that way until the Great Schism in the eleventh century, when the church split over whether or not the Holy Spirit proceeds from the Father or the Father *and* the Son. But there were always, and continue to be, Christian traditions outside the mainstream narrative most of us in the West have been taught, and they all have slightly different beliefs and canons. There is certainly a lot that these traditions share in common, but when we talk about the canon being closed or even about orthodoxy itself, it's important that we remember that Christianity was not and never has been exhausted by the thoughts and traditions of Western Europeans.

Another part of the story that we've been mistaught is the fall of the Roman Empire. It didn't fall.[24] It moved east to Constantinople—modern-day Istanbul, Turkey. This eastern empire became known as the Byzantine Empire. It would eventually lead to the creation of its own distinct Christian tradition, Eastern Orthodoxy, as a result of the Great Schism.

But before that, a critical event happened during the move east. While the Roman Empire didn't crumble, it did lose control over the Nile Delta, and that was a critical moment in biblical history. Why? Because of a plant that flourishes along the Nile: papyrus. Papyrus was plentiful and relatively easy to turn into paper. It was this access to affordable paper that had allowed the written word to flourish, and in the context of Christian history, for so many early Christian texts to be written. Certainly the lack of the sort of central ecclesiastical authority that would follow was an important factor as well in the proliferation of nonorthodox texts in the early centuries of the church, but those texts—heretical or not—would not have been possible or at least as abundant without access to relatively cheap writing materials.

When Rome lost control of Egypt, that source of cheap paper went away, at least for the broader former empire.[25] Which meant copying those early sacred texts—whether orthodox, canonical, or otherwise—became cost prohibitive. Vellum, made from animal skin, replaced papyrus, and vellum was not cheap. It was the sort of stuff only the wealthy could afford, something dedicated to finely crafted texts, not the sort of thing you would casually philosophize or write letters on. As a result, scriptural texts that once were, if not ubiquitous in the early church, at least accessible for a much larger swath of society now became the property of kings and monasteries who could afford them. In other words, Scripture went from the hands of many to the hands of a wealthy or learned few. There was less information for the masses, less material to read about the faith, fewer questions to be asked, and ultimately a loss of personal ownership in their own story because it was simply too expensive to own a copy of Scripture.

For the next thousand years or so, the majority of biblical work involved scribes, typically monks, transcribing and translating the biblical texts they had into Latin, the unifying language of the church. This has led to some popular confusion regarding laity's access to the Bible during the Middle Ages. The popular belief is that the church banned people from reading the Bible, but that is not entirely true.[26] The lack of Bible reading in the Middle Ages is not simply the result of a church trying to control the Bible, but more a matter of education, resources, and access to expensive documents. That's not to say power-hungry folks weren't at work in the church during this period trying to control others through sanctified manipulation. Some certainly were, just as some have, tragically, in every period of the church's history whenever the people (always men) in church power have had to fight to hold onto their power.

However, even if church authorities had been more inclined for laity to read the Bible, it wasn't an option. Most folks didn't read the Bible during the Middle Ages because most people simply could not read. Literacy rates were extremely low during the Middle Ages.[27] Few but the wealthy and clergy could read. Which meant the faithful relied on the preaching of their local bishop or priest to learn the stories and lessons of Scripture. This is also in part why we see so many Bible stories etched into stained glass or carved into stone or painted onto altarpieces during this period. In a world where most people couldn't read the written word, images were the best way to communicate the stories of the Bible to the population.

That's not to say biblical scholarship and important translation work wasn't going on during the so-called Dark Ages. Around 1008 CE the Leningrad Codex was written, a book so named for the library it now calls home in St. Petersburg, Russia, once Leningrad.[28] While you may not have heard of the Leningrad Codex, it is of immense importance, particularly for those of the Jewish faith. It is the oldest complete text that exists of the entire Hebrew Bible in Hebrew (with bits of Aramaic). It is the document from which all modern Jewish translations of the Hebrew Bible are derived, with an intense attention placed on every letter and accent mark because in Jewish tradition God can speak through every letter and accent mark. Even seemingly unrelated passages can be connected and understood through something as simple as a shared accent mark.

It is this Jewish attention to detail that often gets conflated with Christian views of the text in evangelical and fundamentalist circles as proof that biblical texts have an unbroken history of perfect transmission from the very beginning, meaning Christian writers brought the same sort of hyperfocus on the text to make sure every translation and transcription was exactly like the one before.[29] This was not the case. In fact, there is a long history of scribal changes to the biblical text— most pretty minor, but not all. That said, according to biblical scholar Bart Ehrman, there are hundreds of thousands of textual variations across the thousands of copies of the biblical manuscripts that survive today.[30] Most are minor,[31] but it's a large enough number to put a significant dent in any claim that the biblical text we have today has been transmitted perfectly from the moment its writers first put quill to papyrus.

Also happening during this period was a critical change in the formatting of Scripture. The chapter and verse divisions the Bible is so well known for today did not appear in the original manuscripts. Nor were there any punctuation marks. If you were to look at an ancient Greek manuscript, for example, you would see a continuous run-on of letters without the sort of punctuation breaks we use today. The punctuation came later to help clarify the text for readers. And it wasn't until the late twelfth to early thirteenth century that Archbishop Stephen Langdon became the first person to divide the Bible into chapters.[32] It would be another three centuries before the verses we recognize today were inserted into the text by a printer in Paris named Robert Estienne.[33]

Chapters and verses may not seem that big of a deal today. After all, they help us to quickly find passages of scripture we are searching for. But consider for a moment what the effect has been of chopping up what was once a single unit of thought into various subdivisions, the breaks determined by the whims and opinions, however informed they might be, of a handful of people or just one pastor. But we're getting a bit ahead of ourselves. We'll examine those effects later. Let's stay focused on our origin story for right now.

It's tempting to jump straight to the sixteenth century and the Reformation, an incredibly pivotal moment in the history of the Bible. But before we get there it's worth pausing to mention an act that, arguably, helped pave the way for Luther and his fellow Reformers as they sought to get the Bible into the hands of the people. Between 1382 and 1396, an English gentleman by the name of John Wycliffe did something unthinkable, damnable even in the fourteenth century. He translated the Bible from Latin, the language of the church, which most folks couldn't read or speak, into a vernacular language they did speak, English. His reasoning? He wanted more of his fellow Christians to be able to read the Bible for themselves. Sadly, at this point, translating the Bible into the common language of ordinary people wasn't permitted. Low literacy rates were still at play, but church authorities also worried, somewhat justifiably, that the uneducated masses would misunderstand and misconstrue a text that even way back then was well over a thousand years old, and worlds and multiple translated languages away. Whether their concern about interpretation was genuine or simply driven by a more craven desire to maintain control, John Wycliffe's effort to get Scripture into the hands of everyday people was quickly snuffed out.

Wycliffe may not have been as successful as he hoped, but his effort to give the people back their story in their own language would come to fruition just over a century later, when a German monk named Martin Luther arrived on the scene and, well, you know the story. Theses were nailed to a door, a heresy trial was held, and Luther famously told the church authorities demanding he recant, "Hard pass." While on the run from the law and holed up in a castle with nothing better to do, Luther, like Wycliffe, went about translating the Bible into the vernacular of his people—German. Though it's worth noting that had Luther had his way, at least one book of the New Testament would not have made the cut for his translation: the book of James.[34] James declares that faith alone does not save, a decidedly awkward passage for someone whose entire brand was salvation by faith alone.

We need to linger here in the Reformation a moment longer, because another technical revolution took place just before Luther began his revolution. This revolution in technology changed the history of the Bible and its relationship to people every bit as much or more than the shift from affordable papyrus to expensive vellum. The invention of the printing press brought the Bible back into the hands of ordinary people, along with a never-ending flow of religious books, tracts, and pamphlets that were the fuel for both the Reformation and the

Enlightenment that eventually followed. It is not hyperbole to say modern society would not be what it is today without the invention of the printing press. Its effect on the Bible in particular was nearly as profound.

It is during this period that the shift begins from the Bible as the little "w" word of God, the message of God communicated through the story of the people of God, to the big "W" Word of God, wherein the Bible begins to take on an incarnated life of its own as a physical manifestation of the divine, on earth as it is in heaven.[35] That's not to say Protestants suddenly started bowing down to the Bible. They most certainly did not, and they would have been horrified by anyone doing so. But the seeds of the sort of unquestioned adoration fundamentalism has today for the Bible itself can be found here, when the Bible went from the collection of sacred stories and lessons told in church to a cherished representation of the divine in the average household, and a source of both power and authority for rulers across Europe becoming less inclined to bend their knee to the pope.

Whatever control or authority over Scripture the church had once held had been torn apart. In many ways, this was a good thing. But cherished objects have a tendency to become . . . too cherished. The church's control and authority didn't cease with the invention of the printing press. It shifted from the church to the people. The Bible retained its authority, but that authority now resided in the hands of whoever owned a Bible. In turn, those individual Bibles became a source of individual power and authority to be defended at all costs, because while the institutional power of the church may have been waning, the power of Christianity in Europe was still strong. Whoever rightly discerned the meaning of Scripture could command not just a following, but even an entire kingdom.

As the Bible made its way into the hands of everyday people, and they in turn used their newfound power in ways that
terrified long-standing centers of authority, the Roman Catholic Church decided to act. The Council of Trent was first called
in 1545 and held again in 1563. Among other items on the
agenda, the council officially closed the canon for the Roman
Catholic Church.

Now you may be thinking to yourself, "Hold up. I'm confused. I thought the canon was closed centuries before that."
Well yes. . . and no. The canon was effectively closed, pragmatically speaking. Meaning new books or gospels weren't being
produced in hopes of becoming scripture, and the debate was
mostly settled about which books were included. There were,
however, a few outliers and disagreements about a handful of
books, including 1 and 2 Esdras, 1, 2, and 3 Maccabees, and
various other texts held sacred by traditions like the Ethiopian Orthodox Church. This led to different traditions having
slightly different lists of biblical books, which continues to
this day, a curious but important quirk to remember whenever
we talk about "the Bible" as something with a definitive, universally agreed upon definition. But for the Roman Catholic
Church the canon was finally, officially closed at the Council
of Trent.

Not long after the Council of Trent, a new translation of
the Bible was commissioned by the English King James that
would come to dominate the English-speaking world for the
next four hundred years. In 1611 the Authorized Version of
the Bible was published, known today as the King James Version of the Bible. It is hard to overstate its influence not just
on the church but on the English language itself, with many
phrases we now give little thought to finding their origins in
the King James Version: "cast the first stone," "bite the dust,"

"apple of my eye," and "by the skin of my teeth." More than just shaping our modern vernacular, the impact of the King James Bible has been so great that for some Christians today, this translation was and is the definitive and inerrant translation of the Bible—a curious conundrum given that none of the biblical writers spoke English, as it wouldn't exist as a language for more than a millennia after their deaths.[36]

With their new English Bible in hand and a new tradition needing to be legitimized, thanks to King Henry VIII wanting a divorce—and then several more divorces—the Church of England came together in 1646 to produce the Westminster Confession. This document covered a wide range of doctrines, establishing what the Church of England believed on topics such as salvation, the Trinity, and, of course, the Bible. Much like their Catholic counterparts at the Council of Trent, the Church of England's' Westminster Confession also provided an official list of books in the canon, which is the same list used by most Protestant churches today.

The confession is notable for many reasons, but for our purposes it is important to note that this is one of the first official Protestant declarations of what books constitute the Bible, what functions the Bible serves, and the nature of the Bible itself. As we will see later, this is a seminal moment pointed to by many modern adherents of biblical inerrancy as an affirmation of their belief in the Bible being entirely perfect and free from error, though importantly no such claim is made in the Westminster Confession itself.

As England and the rest of Europe began to test the limits of their newfound freedom from ecclesiastical authority, a new quest to understand the world began that led to an explosion of scientific and philosophical inquiry we now call the Enlightenment. The architects of the Enlightenment sought to unlock the mysteries around them in a myriad of ways that didn't include or at least weren't governed by the church or the Bible. However, this new world of intellectual freedom also affected both the church and the Bible and gave rise to so-called higher biblical criticism. This is the sort of biblical inquiry we see today whose focus is not on mining Scripture for polemical support, but rather on the search for better understanding the texts themselves—where they came from, the context out of which they were born, how they were translated, revised, and so on. Put another way, this is when modern biblical scholarship was born, when the study of Scripture ceased to be solely the realm of the pious and began to be explored in a more academic fashion.

There are endless names of important scholars and theologians we could rattle off from the past few centuries of biblical scholarship, but in the story of the Bible, names are less important than a monumental event that happened right around the same time Allied forces were claiming victory in Europe.

As the story goes, the year was 1945 and two young Bedouin boys were out exploring the caves near the Dead Sea when one of them tossed a small rock into a cave. Instead of the expected sound of stone falling on stone, they heard a distinct crashing sound, as if pottery had just broken. Which it had. When the boys went in to explore the source of the unexpected sound, they made one of the greatest archeological discoveries of the twentieth century: scores of clay jars filled with ancient religious texts, including some of our oldest copies of books from the Hebrew Bible.

As professional archaeologists and scavengers alike began to explore the area, they found more caves with more ancient documents, which, it was eventually determined, were likely the creation of a religious sect called the Essenes that lived in a nearby area now called Qumran. The scrolls were and still are some of the most ancient examples of Scripture, specifically the Hebrew Bible, that we have today, dating back to the first century CE. The manuscripts also included documents describing the life and rules of the people who lived in Qumran, giving us better insight into the practice and theology of religious communities during the time of Jesus.

Around the same time that the Dead Sea Scrolls were discovered, the aforementioned treasure trove of ancient gnostic manuscripts was discovered in Nag Hammadi, Egypt. The so-called Nag Hammadi library, like the Dead Sea Scrolls, was discovered by locals. It also revolutionized our understanding of early Christianity, because it contained a small library of early Christian and gnostic writings that gave us a glimpse into the world of Christianity before there was any such thing as orthodoxy, when the first followers of Jesus were still trying to figure out exactly who he was and what the implications of his life, death, and resurrection were for themselves and the rest of the world.

While certainly the most famous discoveries of the past century, the Dead Sea Scrolls and the Nag Hammadi library are far from the only ancient manuscripts and scraps of ancient copies of Scripture that have made it into the hands of scholars. Those pieces that have been discovered, rediscovered, translated, and compared have created much better and more accurate translations of the Bible. This is for the simple reason that, odd as it may sound, we have access to better and older documents than, for example, the translators of the King James Bible four hundred years ago.

As a result, the past century has seen an explosion of different translations in both the English-speaking and non-English-speaking world, with various traditions, denominations, and

scholars preferring differing translations. Some because they
are a more literal translation of the original, others because
they make for better reading, and still others because the
translation better adheres to a tradition's theological emphasis (something seen most often today in battles over gendered
pronouns both for God and the people of God).

You can also find Bibles packaged in an endless variety of
Bible study themes for just about any demographic out there.
There are study Bibles for men, women, teens, kids, soldiers,
comic book lovers, hunters, patriots, and everyone else in
between. Whoever you are, wherever you might be, whatever
interests you might have, there is almost certainly a Bible out
there custom-made to your particular tastes. It's an inspired
act of marketing that lets each of us tell the story of the people
of God however we best see fit.

Regardless of what translation or edition of the Bible, if any,
you choose to read, the fact that it exists at all and is still so
revered is nothing short of a miracle. That a somewhat unified
group was able to emerge from the chaos and confusion of the
earliest days of the church and then generally agree upon a list
of sacred writing was nothing short of a miracle that speaks
to the hand of the Spirit at work—not dictating the life of the
early church, but rather guiding its formation while leaving
space for human perspective, diversity, interest, and need. But
come together the canon did. Not in dark, nefarious ways,
but in common shared opinion that these books, rather than
other books—and there were many other books and gospels
during that early period—best told the story of the people of
God and were pragmatically the most helpful in living out the
way of Jesus.

What we see in the life of the early church isn't a magical process of the Bible falling from heaven, orthodoxy being

dictated from the sky, or churches forming *ex nihilo* in their final form. What we see are real people with real diversity of thought, opinion, and practice trying to figure it out on the fly. They worked together and sometimes fought one another but were all trying to understand the same mystery: who exactly is this guy from Nazareth, and what does it mean that his tomb is empty? This was the truth they were trying to understand, the story they were trying to tell.

The questions were simple enough, but the answers were many, and the earliest followers of Jesus fought over them just as we continue to fight theological battles today. The idea of a golden era of the church where everyone got along happily, agreed on everything, and never squabbled is an illusion not even the Bible itself tries to maintain. They were people working out their faith just as we continue to work out our faith today. And it was out of this working out of the faith by different groups of people in different corners of the Mediterranean, with traditions and ideas and beliefs as unique as the places they came from, that the New Testament began to emerge.

It's important to understand this process because it is the context in which the entire Bible was actually written. It helps us see why the Bible, even when compiled over a relatively short period of time as the New Testament was, can have so many different and even divergent and contradictory ideas within its pages. The Bible is the story of the people of God told by the people of God. Inspired to be sure, but when we strip away or reduce the role of humanity to something akin to data entry, we lose or at least miss what makes the Bible so remarkable and, well, so inspiring.

The writers of the Bible were inspired to write their stories because those stories had inspired them. By writing those stories down they ensured they wouldn't be lost, that the inspiration would continue long after they were gone. That new generations not yet conceived would find the same divine inspiration the original writers found in the stories of God at work in the lives of God's people. These weren't just entertaining stories or cold, ruthless laws. They were the Spirit at work, revealing good news and inspiring the people of God to live out the sort of lives they were created for. And in so doing to spread that inspiration throughout the world, not just through words on a page, but through lives inspired by those words made flesh in the lives and actions of the faithful.

This is the sort of inspiration the Spirit is up to in the world. It is quite literally an in-Spirit-ing act. That is to say, true inspiration—biblical inspiration—is the Spirit of God coming to dwell within us and within our world. God isn't interested in simply writing a good book or even a collection of good books that entertain readers and give them warm, fuzzy feelings. By inspiring the writers of the Bible, God is extending an invitation to its readers to join with God and the people of God to remake creation into the sort of place God imagined when God separated light from darkness and dirt from water with a word. Those inspired stories become the sort of stuff a holy imagination is made of, the kind of mind shaped by the breath of God to see the world not just how it is but how it could be, even how it should be. This is the sort of inspiration that breathes life into the reader, who then becomes inspired to share that breath of life with others, thereby creating a sort of holy ecosystem wherein we work together to thrive and spread good news and support one another, imagining and incarnating a new world in the here and now.

It's this ongoing kinetic activity that makes the Bible a living document—not a book or even just a library, but an active storytelling workshop, an ongoing anthology that invites the reader to continue the work of telling the story of the people of God. That doesn't mean we're called to write new books for the Bible, at least not in the same way Isaiah, Mark, or Paul did. Rather, we're called to tell the story of God's people by retelling the stories of the Bible and by telling new stories of our own, both in word and deed, about how God continues to work in the world making all things new. The Bible inspires us, breathes into us the divine breath of life through the Holy Spirit, so that we will be inspired—infilled with the Spirit—to go and breathe that life into the world.

Inspiration isn't the end point of Scripture, though we often treat it that way, as if the point of Scripture is to prove it's inspired, or more extremely, altogether perfect. The point of affirming the inspiration of Scripture is found in being inspired to inspire others, in living out the good news so that others might see God's light shining through us and want to take their seat alongside us at the table of God. When that is our goal—building out the heavenly community rather than just winning a debate or performatively affirming dogma—the Bible presents us with a new challenge, one grounded not in winning arguments, but in finding in the Scriptures we believe to be inspired by God a meaning worthy of the God we believe it portrays.

When finding a meaning worthy of God is our guide for reading, interpreting, and implementing Scripture, so many of the ways we formerly used the Bible become nonstarters. Beating others over the head with clobber passages and damning them to hell because they don't agree with our interpretation, no matter how plain we might think it is, is not a meaning worthy of a loving God. It's not inspiring to anyone, and it is certainly not life-giving. It's the sort of calcification that destroys our Spirit-breathed imagination and brings death to all who accidentally find themselves in our zealous wake.

The biblical writers wrote down their stories and poems and songs and letters and gospels because they saw in them a story worth telling, a story of hope and inspiration and grace, of love and life and community, that was worth putting pen to paper to share with the world. Closing the canon doesn't mean we should close our hearts and minds to what God continues to do. Our task as readers of those stories is to find in them a meaning worthy of God, a meaning worthy of the One who created out of love, a story worth belonging to and a life worth living.

3

BORN AGAIN ON
THE BOARDWALK

The Bible became perfect on September 16, 1835.

Okay, maybe not that day exactly, but that's when its evolution to perfection began. On the sixteenth day of September 1835, after four years at sea, a twenty-two-year-old English scientist first set foot on a chain of remote islands off the coast of South America. He had been hired as a geologist but was eager to get his hands on samples of anything interesting he could find, whether it be rock, bird, or budding flower.

His name was Charles Darwin, and what he found on the Galapagos Islands would forever change not just the foundation of science, but also the Bible and its role in the church and among society writ large. Darwin didn't set out to change the Bible or how anyone in the church understood it. When he first set foot on the rocky shores of the Galapagos, he wasn't looking to start a revolution. But fourteen years later when he finally published *On the Origin of Species*, its impact was felt nearly every bit as much in the church as it was in the classroom.

Before Darwin began studying the finches of the Galapagos, biblical critics born in the fires of the Enlightenment had begun to cast doubt on the accuracy of the Bible. These were folks who weren't necessarily in awe of the Bible as the source of all knowledge the way that clergy and the faithful were. With the shackles of ecclesiastical dogma cast off, so-called higher criticism had arisen as an offshoot of the Enlightenment's quest to better understand the world. Biblical scholars began asking hard questions and looking past long-held assumptions about things like the authorship of various books of the Bible, their composition, context, and historical accuracy. But that movement didn't come close to igniting the spark of revolution the way Darwin's theory of evolution did.

The biblical critics or scholars were mildly annoying to clergy and laypeople alike with their doubts and questions, but to many clergy and laity, Darwin's work was a direct, full-throated, and not-so-easily dismissed assault on both the Bible and the very idea of where we came from and how the world came to be. That's not to say there weren't folks who didn't buy into a six-thousand-year-old Earth theory before Darwin came along. Plenty of people didn't read the first chapters of Genesis literally, including countless rabbis and even early church fathers like Augustine, who wrote way back in the fourth century CE that anyone who took the Genesis account of creation literally was a fool.[1] Some folks heeded his warning, many did not. Those that didn't were in for a rude awakening when Darwin finally arrived on the scene.

To say some clergymen were upset about Darwin's thesis that the forces of natural selection and evolution were responsible for our present existence, rather than God literally breathing into a pile of dirt, would be an understatement. Had burnings at the stake still been allowed, many church folks probably would have turned Darwin into burnt toast along with every copy of Origin of Species they could find. But they couldn't do that, so they did the next best thing. They deemed evolution a heresy, damned Darwin to hell, and then got to work formulating the rest of the response.[2]

They weren't scientists themselves, so offering up an alternative scientific explanation wasn't an option. But they were authorities on the Bible. Or had been invested with authority on the Bible. Or at least had given it to themselves. So they put that authority to work to try to prove Darwin wrong. Of course, that wouldn't be a straightforward effort, as the Bible is not the sort of scientific textbook that Darwin wrote, nor does it address any of the specific theories of evolution that Darwin raised. But the Bible did offer an alternative account of the origin of our species, and that was good enough. Sure, it wasn't an account that the Jewish community who wrote it necessarily took as literal, but that didn't matter.[3] There was power and authority to maintain. Rather than a myth or poem or declaration of the creative love of God, the Bible and its account of creation had to become something more if it was going to stand up to the perceived threat of science.

The faithful already believed the Bible to be the ultimate source of truth, but Darwin's work revealed a flaw in their armor. He gave a detailed explanation for how the natural world came to be the way we see it today. It was an explanation that could not be easily ignored because on its face it seemed to contradict the book of Genesis and, in turn, seemed to leave no room for a Creator in creation. So in the face of a mountain of evidence, many of the faithful followed the tried and true path of every child who has ever been told they're wrong and knew they were wrong, but didn't want to believe it. They plugged their ears and declared: the Bible says it, I believe it, that settles it.

Of course just saying "I believe it. That settles it" wasn't enough. The Bible had lost some of its authority outside the doors of the church. It needed a prophetic refill. And this time there couldn't be anything left to chance lest the church lose its place as the supreme repository of truth and authority in the world. The best way to insure the Bible against another Darwin was to declare that it couldn't possibly be wrong about anything because it was perfect in every way. It wasn't just the story of the people of God. It was the very words of God himself. It was inerrant, perfect in every way, and anyone who disagreed—anyone who had the gall to question its science, history, anthropology, cosmology, or ethics—was a heretic damned to hell.

It was a deceptively simple, but powerful, defense. After all, few things get folks back in line quicker than telling them they're on the path to eternal damnation. Why was the Bible perfect? Because they said so, or more accurately because they said it said so. The reasoning was a perfect circle that left no space for questioning or doubt. Forget questions about science. Questions, like doubt itself, were now damnable because the Bible was perfect and therefore beyond any doubt or questioning. Its perfection must simply be accepted. Period.

And really, who could blame them for reacting this way? If your salvation rests on faith alone, you can't risk putting your faith in ideas that are anything but perfect in every way. Inerrancy wasn't just a quirky theological dispute. It was an essential defense of the faith, the very key to salvation itself.

Now the folks who invented inerrancy and certainly the folks who profess it today would tell you that inerrancy is as old as Christianity itself.[4] That it is core orthodoxy, and fundamentalists were just putting words and affirmation to what the church has always believed. But had it really? Inerrancy may be on the lips of conservative and fundamentalist Christians today, but it's both a word and idea that doesn't appear anywhere in the history of the church before the late nineteenth to early twentieth century. That's not to say folks didn't have a high, even extremely high, view of Scripture before then. They very much did. But the idea of the Bible being utterly flawless in every way, including its accounts of science and history, is a thoroughly modern idea, not least because the modern science to which so much of fundamentalism is reacting is, as the name implies, modern.

This nascent push for inerrancy was a modern response to the rise of higher biblical criticism, which cast down long-held assumptions about the Bible and its credibility. Again, this was not the case for every Christian of the time. Many embraced Darwin's ideas or at the very least didn't view evolution as an existential threat to Christianity and the Bible.[5] Unfortunately, their forces tended to be drowned out by the cries of the fundamentalist mob.

The folks who did view Darwin and his theory of evolution as an existential threat to the faith have collectively come to be known as fundamentalists because of their adherence to certain beliefs about the Christian faith that they believed were essential or fundamental to Christian orthodoxy, and with it, salvation itself. Though fundamentalists themselves were not, nor do they remain, a monolithic group. There are a number of theological matters about which fundamentalists disagree. But they do agree, or at least mostly agree, on what they believe are the fundamental tenets of Christianity.

Coined in 1920, the name *fundamentalists* was drawn from the publication of several pamphlets or essays entitled *The Fundamentals*.[6] Published between 1910 and 1915, *The Fundamentals* was commissioned by a California oilman by the name of Lyman Stuart. Stuart, along with his brother Milton, sought to provide a defense of the faith for the faithful, or at least the faithful who believed as they did that the Bible was perfect, indisputable truth.[7]

While a literal interpretation of the Bible is the thing most closely associated with fundamentalism today, *The Fundamentals* listed several beliefs that were no longer up for debate in the Christian faith, because their adherents believed they were the foundation of the faith and without them the faith would fall apart. Along with the trustworthiness of Scripture, which, perhaps surprisingly, didn't appear until volume two, *The Fundamentals* included essays on such theological topics as the virgin birth, the deity of Christ, various attacks on higher criticism, an emphasis on justification by faith alone, and several personal testimonies to attest to the truthfulness and importance of what was being said. Altogether this collection totaled ninety essays printed over the first half of the 1910s. So important were they to the ideological formation of fundamentalism that they remain in print today, over a century after their initial publication.

These essays were but the opening salvo in the war to defend the Bible from its attackers. While the writers of *The Fundamentals* were hard at work writing their essays, the Presbyterian Church in America was meeting in Atlantic City for their General Assembly. Whatever else may have been discussed and debated over the course of the assembly, the lasting legacy of the convention was the affirmation of what would become known as the Five Fundamentals: (1) the inspiration and inerrancy of Scripture, (2) the virgin birth, (3) substitutionary atonement, (4) the bodily resurrection of Jesus, and (5) the historicity of biblical miracles, meaning the belief that all biblical miracles happened literally in history.[8] There wasn't much that was particularly new about any of these beliefs, except the first one. While *The Fundamentals* essays were being written at the same time, they were an independent work, not something commissioned by any denomination. The affirmation of the Five Fundamentals, however, was an official act of a denomination, and as such it became the first time in the history of the Christian church that biblical inerrancy was declared to be an official part of church orthodoxy, or at least Presbyterian orthodoxy.

Given the emphasis fundamentalism places on biblical inerrancy as a core element of historical Christian orthodoxy, it's worth emphasizing the point that biblical inerrancy appears in no creed or confession of any denomination or church council before 1910. Perhaps you might be thinking to yourself, they were just formalizing something that had long been believed and assumed. While "long held" is a generous description of that particular doctrine's legacy, Christian orthodoxy doesn't operate on unspoken assumptions. We list and confess our core beliefs. We write them down and declare them in church. For example, there is no more fundamental and assumed doctrine of Christian orthodoxy than the crucifixion and resurrection of Jesus. Those twin beliefs are so assumed as central to the faith that even most non-Christians recognize their fundamental importance to the church, and yet they have been confessed in creedal form and affirmed by church council from the very dawn of Christianity.

Which means if the church suddenly affirms a new doctrine as orthodoxy, it is not because it was accidentally overlooked in the previous two thousand years or assumed so obvious no one thought to bother bringing it up. Christians have debated the minutiae of even the most abstract theology for centuries. Inerrancy wasn't overlooked. It was simply never officially affirmed or thought of as orthodoxy by any creed or council until the Presbyterians made it so on the boardwalk of Atlantic City in 1910.[9]

But Presbyterians were far from the only Christians in America caught up in the fervor of fundamentalism. Fundamentalism was deeply attractive to a wide swath of Christians genuinely concerned about the rapidly changing world around them. Fundamentalism gave them both an anchor to hold onto as the world around them changed and the reassurance that what they had always believed to be true was still true. As a movement, fundamentalism exploded across the United States in the early part of the twentieth century. This culminated in a movement spurred by fundamentalists to pass new laws banning what could be taught in public schools, particularly Darwin's dangerous theory of evolution. Worried that evolutionary theory would undermine the faith of their children and transform them into godless liberals, activists worked to ban the teaching of evolution in classrooms across the country.[10]

Of course, not all Christians were on board with the rise of fundamentalism. Other evangelicals in traditions and denominations now referred to as mainline spoke out against the paranoia of fundamentalism. One pastor in particular gave an urgent cry to action from his pulpit in a sermon that still echoes to this day. His name was Harry Emerson Fosdick, pastor of the prominent First Presbyterian Church in New York City. In his now famous sermon *Shall the Fundamentalists Win?* Fosdick challenged the American church not to surrender to the hysteria whipped up by fundamentalism and instead to create a big tent for Christians of various stripes to come together to agree and disagree without damning each other to hell over abstract dogma. Fosdick asked, "Has anybody a right to deny the Christian name to those who differ with him on such points and to shut against them the doors of the Christian fellowship?"[11] Though intentionally welcoming in tone, Fosdick drew a sharp contrast between openness to science, to learning, growing, and discovering new ways of seeing and understanding the world, and fundamentalism's close-minded mentality of having everything already figured out.

Fosdick was challenging the church to tell a better story than the fundamentalists. A story free from fear and on-demand damnation. A story of hope and liberation, of wonder and possibility. A story worth believing in. But to those happy with the way things were and afraid of what change could bring, Fosdick's sermon wasn't a rallying cry. It was a harbinger of what was to come if liberalism made its way into the doors of the church. And so, not long after his iconic sermon, Fosdick was forced out of his church. Fortunately for him, he had a friend named John Rockefeller who had the tithe money to build Fosdick a new church called Riverside where he could continue his ministry in peace.

But not everyone was so lucky in the battle of fundamentalism in America. Fundamentalists in Tennessee successfully lobbied their state legislature to pass a law banning the teaching of evolution in Tennessee classrooms to protect the children from dangerous theories they viewed as critical of their faith.[12] John Scopes, a teacher in rural Rhea County in southeast Tennessee, politely said thanks but no thanks to the state's offer to keep his students living in scientific ignorance. Scopes defied the state ban, taught evolution, and quickly found himself on the wrong side of the law, arrested and sent to court for what would become one of the most notorious trials of the twentieth century.

The so-called Monkey Trial captured the nation's attention like few legal cases before or since. It brought two of the most prominent attorneys in the country to Dayton, Tennessee, to fight it out in a made-for-TV trial before TV had even been invented. Press from around the country descended on

Dayton. The courtroom was filled to capacity with people eager to listen to Clarence Darrow and William Jennings Bryan rhetorically duke it out for the future of public education and the soul of a nation. With no Netflix to chill to, Americans waited with bated breath for every radio and newspaper update coming from Tennessee. Unfortunately for Mr. Scopes, he did not enjoy a Hollywood ending. He was found guilty and fined one hundred dollars. On appeal, Scopes was acquitted—not due to the unconstitutionality of the law, however, but because the fine was deemed too excessive.

Not long after the fundamentalists won their day in court, another battle began to brew on the campus of one of the preeminent and most influential seminaries in the country— Princeton Theological Seminary. This time it was a fight over control between old school conservatives who fought to defend the teaching of inerrancy and new school moderates who were less persuaded by the truth of the doctrine their colleagues were so passionate about. After back-and-forth debates and input from Presbyterian General Assembly committees, the so-called New School moderates won out and the Old School conservatives left to form their own seminary.[13] They named it Westminster Theological Seminary, a name chosen to prove their allegiance to the Westminster Confession, a critical document for Reformed theology and one that biblical inerrantists would place a lot of weight on when arguing for the historicity of biblical inerrancy. This despite, once again, the confession making no direct mention of biblical inerrancy.

Though they could claim some victory between Princeton and Dayton, the early days of the twentieth century were something of a mixed bag for fundamentalists. While they may have won the day in court and even started their own seminary, they had—at least for the moment—lost the battle of public opinion.

In choosing a rural town in Tennessee as their battleground, and a straight-from-central-casting bombastic lawyer as their representative, fundamentalists inadvertently succeeded in portraying themselves as the very caricatures their critics maligned them as being.[14] The sheen of their righteous zeal to save the children from critical theory was lost and fundamentalism receded into the shadows.[15] Unfortunately, it was a retreat to reinforce, not a total surrender. Though bruised and battered, the fundamentalists were not defeated. Over the next several decades they slowly but surely got to work planning their return to public life and the takeover of American Christianity they believed they were called to achieve for the sake of their neighbors' salvation.

The first battle in what would become a decades-long fundamentalist siege took place about as far away from the mountains of Tennessee as you can get. Founded by conservative evangelicals in 1947 just a short drive from the beaches of southern California, Fuller Theological Seminary became a testing ground in the 1960s for fundamentalists to see how far they could go in forcing their theological priorities on the greater evangelical educational system and eventually the church itself. The long and short of the source of this theological squabble came down to a clause affirming biblical inerrancy in a document professors were obligated to sign in order to teach at the seminary. Eventually, the affirmation of biblical inerrancy was removed. Disagreeing professors left and on their way out denounced the still conservative evangelical seminary as a hotbed of liberal godlessness.[16] The now unemployed professors found new jobs in new seminaries around the country created with the express intent of upholding and affirming the fundamentals of the faith—most importantly, biblical inerrancy.

The importance of this maneuvering cannot be overstated. Even if they don't always see eye to eye, congregations are led, taught, and influenced in their faith in critical ways by their pastors. And even if those pastors don't always see eye to eye with their professors, those pastors are led, taught, and influenced in their faith in critical ways by them in seminary. So if someone can shape the seminary in such a way that the professors are all on the same or close to the same fundamentalist page, you can create generations of pastors who take that fundamentalist theology and spread it to the masses as Christian orthodoxy in a way no campaign, pamphlet, law, or trial ever could.

So what was once a fringe movement slowly became orthodoxy in the minds of countless Christians, pastors, professors, and laity alike as the first generation of fundamentalists died off and those that remained couldn't remember a time when inerrancy wasn't affirmed as orthodoxy. It was both an echo chamber of ideas and a grassroots movement that proved incredibly effective. So much so that it laid the groundwork for the fundamentalist takeover of the largest Protestant denomination in the United States—the Southern Baptist Convention. That groundwork for the fundamentalist takeover of the SBC and conservative evangelicalism in general was put in place by the so-called Chicago Statement. Its creation was headed by pastor and theologian R. C. Sproul, who initially reached out to the editor of *Christianity Today* to hold a conference affirming biblical inerrancy. When the magazine declined his invitation, Sproul created his own convention called the International Council on Biblical Inerrancy. Held over several days in October 1978 in Chicago, Illinois, the conference brought together more than three hundred pastors, scholars, and theologians to create a statement affirming the doctrine of biblical inerrancy as indisputable Christian orthodoxy.[17]

The Chicago Statement may not be one you are familiar with, but it has had profound influence on conservative evangelicalism ever since. It has served as a sort of theological anchor for contemporary fundamentalists in the midst of criticism from other biblical scholars and Christian laity who do not share the convictions of those three hundred self-appointed men meeting together in a hotel ballroom. But that anchor has held strong, with its most immediate impact coming through its influence on the fundamentalist takeover of the Southern Baptist Convention, a conquest that by virtue of the convention's sheer size would have widespread influence not just on Baptist churches but American evangelicalism as a whole.[18]

It might sound strange today, especially given that the denomination was established on the basis that slavery was clearly a divinely ordained institution (a position they did not formally renounce of until 1995),[19] but the Southern Baptist Convention was not always the bastion of Christian fundamentalism that it is today. The denomination we know today came about through the determined work of a number of groups and individuals intentionally working to move the denomination more in line with their preferred fundamentalist theology. According to the ecclesiastical conquistadors themselves,

> The SBC came up with a game plan to win back their seminaries and denomination from its drift away from this fundamental pillar of the Christian faith. It was not easy, and the road was long, but the result has proved the wisdom of their plan. The plan included recruiting delegates from the churches to vote for inerrancy-believing presidents who were prominent pastors in the SBC (including Adrian Rogers, Charles Stanley, Jimmy Draper, Bailey Smith, and

Ed Young). Once these men were elected presidents by a vote of the delegates, they in turn appointed persons to crucial positions in the denomination, who in turn appointed board members in the seminaries. Once they had a majority on the boards, they could hire inerrantist presidents and deans, who were then able to hire inerrantist faculty and turn the schools around . . . Within a few decades the inerrantists were able to control their seminaries again and build a foundation on inerrant Scripture.[20]

With all the pieces on the board, fundamentalists were now in a strong position to ensure their theology was passed on to the next generation of evangelicals as indisputable Christian orthodoxy. But to ensure that future, they needed to document a theological past that stretched back further than the 1970s and the statement they themselves had written. So the conquistadors got to work. Because they sincerely believed inerrancy was a doctrine as old as the Christian faith itself, mining church history for proof was for these fundamentalists something akin to proving the sky is blue. The evidence, in their minds, was abundant and indisputable. All they needed to do was collect it.

So that's what they did, as they began to pore through the writings of the church fathers and Reformation heroes to prove that biblical inerrancy was something the church has always affirmed, even if it was never mentioned in such a way—not least because the Bible as we know it didn't even exist when the early church fathers were writing about what would become canonized as holy scripture. Moreover, had they delved a bit deeper into the history of the early church, fundamentalists probably would not have liked what they found there: inclusiveness, creativity, women in ministry, little central authority, and only basic dogma.

But fundamentalism has never let facts get in the way of a good story and reappropriating church history was a smart and essential tactic. You can't appeal to historical tradition without a history, and when that history hasn't been written for you, you write it yourself. So, willingly or not, many of the great writers of Christian history were rebaptized as biblical inerrantists.

Among the church fathers conscripted for the cause was Irenaeus, who once wrote, "The Scriptures are indeed perfect, since they were spoken by the Word of God and His Spirit."[21] There was also Origen, who professed, "In the two testaments every word that pertains to God may be required and discussed, and all knowledge of things may be understood out of them."[22] The great Augustine wrote, "Of all the books of the world, I believe that only the authors of holy Scripture were totally free from error, and if I am puzzled by anything in them that seems to go against the truth, I do not hesitate to suppose that either the manuscript is faulty or the translator has not caught the sense of what was said, or I have failed to understand it for myself."[23] Continuing their march through church history, a reformer like Martin Luther also found himself conscripted for the cause of inerrancy, having once written: "I have learned to ascribe the honor of infallibility only to those books that are accepted as canonical. I am profoundly convinced that none of these writers has erred."[24]

Bereft of any context, these quotes make the case for a long tradition of inerrancy seem very strong. When we pay no attention to anything else the conscripted theologians said or did and ignore the inherent anachronism of the Bible not existing in the first couple centuries of the early church, the case for inerrancy appears almost airtight. But the fundamentalists didn't stop there.

The argument for a tradition of inerrancy was further pushed by an appeal to the 1646 Westminster Confession, one of the first great formal declarations of the Protestant faith. As discussed in chapter 2, the confession lent legitimacy to the Church of England, created by Henry VIII on the occasion of his desire for a divorce. It also laid down many basic tenets of faith and practice for the newly formed tradition. Among these tenets was a statement on Holy Scripture which affirms, "All which are given by inspiration of God to be the rule of faith and life," and "The authority of the Holy Scripture, for which it ought to be believed, and obeyed, dependeth not upon the testimony of any man, or church; but wholly upon God (who is truth itself) the author thereof: and therefore it is to be received, because it is the Word of God."[25] The confession also declares, "Our full persuasion and assurance of the infallible truth and divine authority thereof, is from the inward work of the Holy Spirit."[26] Once again, when you come to the confession assuming it says what you want it to say, this seems like strong support for inerrancy.

Surprisingly, however, the Westminster Confession doesn't support the more modern emphasis on the Bible always having a clear and plain meaning: "All things in Scripture are not alike plain in themselves, nor alike clear unto all."[27] That clarity, the confession says, is reserved for "those things which are necessary to be known, believed, and observed for salvation."[28] The closest we come to an argument for infallibility in the Westminster Confession is a moment of sanctified circular reasoning toward the end of the section on Scripture, which reads "The infallible rule of interpretation of Scripture is the Scripture itself."[29] It is important to note that *infallibility* is here referring to a method of interpretation, not necessarily to Scripture itself. One could, and many do, make the leap to argue that in order for Scripture to be infallible at interpreting itself it must itself first be infallible, but that is not necessarily the case, and in any case it is not what the confession affirms.

In fact, the modern idea of inerrancy, of a Bible free of all error and both historically and scientifically accurate in all ways, is not found anywhere in the Westminster Confession. You can perhaps see the building blocks of such an idea, but to declare this proof of a tradition of inerrancy is asking more of the document than it can provide.

While the evidence for historical inerrancy from the time of the Reformation and the events that followed in its wake may not be as strong as fundamentalists would like, we do see a curious and important shift during this period of ecclesiastical revolution that does add to the tradition of inerrancy. Namely, the aforementioned transition of the Bible from being the little "w" word of God to becoming the big "W" Word of God. As we've seen, the timing makes sense. The Reformation leaned heavily on the Bible to make its case for overthrowing the authority of the Catholic Church. It needed divine authority to usurp divine authority, and with the invention of the printing press that authority could now be found in the pocket of anyone who could afford to buy a Bible.

However, the Bible became not just affordable, but an essential weapon of revolution. Not just its message, but the book itself became a holy weapon of war. The message of God's word became the Word made flesh in print and ink—a designation that previously had been reserved for Jesus alone. The Bible had to become divine if *sola scriptura*, the doctrine of Scripture alone as the church's guide, was to be true. Without a divine Word the church would be lost. The Bible had always been a guide alongside the church, but it now became *the* guide. The word became the Word. The great irony of this theological revolution is that though they professed *sola scriptura* and made claims of plain and clear meanings, the Protestant Reformers immediately splintered into factions based on whose plain and clear interpretation was actually correct.[30]

That splintering continues to this very day. While there may be no debate in fundamentalist circles today about whether or not the Bible is inerrant, the battle over whose *sola scriptura* interpretation of that perfect text continues unabated. It may seem trivial, but for many professing Christians, this story of biblical perfection isn't just worth believing in, it's essential. Without a perfect Bible, the fear is we are also left without a reliable witness to the gospel, and without a reliable gospel from which we draw our understanding of how to be saved, how can we be assured of our salvation? Whether you affirm inerrancy or not, this concern is understandable, at least in the context of fundamentalist Protestantism that rests firmly on the doctrine of *sola fide*, the belief that we are saved from the fires of hell through faith alone. If you believe you face the potential of an eternity being tortured in hell based on faith alone, you want to be sure you're confessing the right faith and you want to know the source of that faith can be trusted. You want a perfect Bible so you can sleep at night knowing you have nothing to fear if for some reason you don't wake up or Jesus returns in the middle of the night.

If you didn't grow up in this world, it can be hard to understand just how much this fear of hell drives so much of Christianity in general—not just fundamentalism. If you did grow up in the fundamentalist bubble, it can be equally hard to understand how this fear doesn't consume someone's every waking hour.

The bubble around the fundamentalist ecosphere is intentionally airtight, hermetically sealed off from all influence from the outside world. It has to be to maintain the illusion of being the chosen ones entrusted with God's truth. The bubble is not just going to church every Sunday and Wednesday. It's home Bible studies, mission trips, Christian music, Christian sports leagues, Christian movies, Christian activities of every kind so that everyone you know is a Christian, everything you experience is Christian, and everything you learn comes from Christian sources. Eventually you begin to believe that your particular form of Christianity isn't just the right form of Christianity, it's normative of life in general, and anyone can be led to believe that those who are not just like you are either lost or the enemy.

Fundamentalism, then, isn't just a mindset or a theology. It's a way of life. A safe harbor in the midst of a rapidly changing and sometimes scary world. It's an attempt to carve out the kingdom of God on earth as it is in heaven—which makes those things listed by fundamentalists as fundamental and essential to the faith so curious, not because of what they include but what they don't. Among the affirmation of a perfect Bible, the need for salvation, and the resurrection of Jesus as fundamental and essential to the Christian faith, one fundamental thing is often conspicuously missing.

Love.

4

ICARUS

Growing up, my favorite Sundays were testimony Sundays. Well, that and the time someone forgot to get the standard wafers for communion and we ended up using dinner rolls from the bakery down the street, but that was a one-time miracle. (Rest in peace, Sunbeam Bakery.) Testimony Sundays were a regular thing at my church, but they weren't always planned. Planned or not, they meant a break from hearing the preacher preach his sermon, and there is no preacher alive that can hold the attention of an eight-year-old for forty-five minutes. Since I never knew they were going to happen when they did, walking into a testimony Sunday was like waking up on Christmas morning, except instead of He-Man toys, my gift was not having to listen to a long sermon.

On testimony Sundays, my family would show up for church just like any other Sunday morning. I would settle into the pew with my coloring book and the preacher would stand in front of the pulpit to announce he wouldn't be preaching that day.[1] Instead, he would be opening the floor to anyone and everyone who had a testimony to share about what God was doing in their lives. People would pop up one after another as a mic was passed, sometimes not quickly enough, so that anxious testifiers began testifying before the mic was in their hand and the congregation was left wondering what exactly it was that God was responding to in their lives.

Nevertheless, they would share whatever it was they wanted to share—typically good news, but not always—and then sit down to let the next person testify. This would go on for at least the same amount of time allotted for the preacher's sermon, but often went well over, because once you open the floor for testimony time it's hard, if not downright sinful, to tell people you've run out of time and they can't share what God is doing in their lives.

Those Sundays when things dragged on too long and cut into lunch were frustrating for young me, but they were balanced out by super surprise testimony Sundays. I say super surprise because not even the pastor knew these testimony Sundays were going to happen. On these occasions, the pastor would start his sermon, proclaim something that really moved someone to the point they felt compelled to stand up, interrupt the preacher, and start talking about whatever it was they felt God had laid on their heart to share. Sometimes this would be just one person with a super surprise testimony. They would stand up, do their thing, and the pastor would go back to preaching, leaving young me crestfallen at the prospect of what always felt like an eternity of preaching. But other times, many times in fact, that first super surprise testimony was like the falling of small stones that starts an avalanche in the mountains. The first testifier would sit down and before the preacher could say, "Thank you for that, now where were we . . . " someone else stood up and then another and another. All the while I was bent over in my pew praying as fervently as a saint that the testimonies would continue till the end of service. But no later, obviously. Otherwise we would be stuck waiting an hour to get a table at Longhorn.

If that all sounds a bit strange or even unsettling to you, then you obviously didn't grow up in the sort of Pentecostally-adjacent evangelicalism I did.[2] That's okay. I forgive you. None of us can be blamed for where we were born. But while you may not have experienced spontaneous testimony time on Sunday morning, if you grew up in the church, any church, chances are that personal testimonies were still—in one form or another—an important part of whatever tradition you were raised in. Because aside from being a welcome distraction for children, testifying to what God has done in the lives of the people of God is an important part of church life. It is, not just in effect, but quite literally, what the Bible is all about and why it exists at all. It's the story of what God has done in the lives of the people of God.

We don't testify just to testify. We don't tell stories just to tell stories. And we don't write scripture just to have a reliable source of Hobby Lobby decorations. We are a story-formed people who share the stories of God at work in our lives because it is in those stories that we find truth. Not just any truth, but *the* Truth, the Logos of God at work in the world informing and shaping us into the people we were created to be.

When we tell the stories of God at work in our lives, we join with the ancient story of the people of God that has been told since God first breathed into a pile of dirt to create humanity. But we don't just tell the stories of God at work in the world—we live them out through every act of hopeful defiance in the face of injustice, through compassion in a world of greed, through showing grace when it's needed most, and through inclusion when the stranger is being rejected. Christianity isn't about telling the truth, it's about living it. And so is the Bible.

Which is why if we locate truth only in the historical details of our stories, we miss where the Truth really lies. That's not to say God acting in history isn't important. It is, and God does. That is why we tell our stories of faith. Not just in hopeful anticipation that God will act again one day, but as proof that God has acted before. It's not the sort of evidence you find in an FBI lab or even a philosophical debate, but the sort of proof that has to be experienced, breathed in, cried through, and celebrated over. Unfortunately, we've been conditioned to believe that truth can only be told through historically verifiable accounts. That divorced from documentable archeology, a story becomes myth, and myths are not truth. But that couldn't be further from, well, the truth.

The problem is with our understanding of truth. We too often relegate truth to a list of facts, like a scientific catalog to be mined whenever we need to prove a point or damn someone to hell. This is why fundamentalism is so fundamentally tied to literalism. It's a list of facts to memorize, not a story to tell. But the truth of the Bible isn't found in a set of facts or even simply in its saving message. Nor does its message rest on, or depend upon, every other statement being objectively factual and historically provable, as if perfection were a necessary precondition for communicating truth. You and I have spent our entire lives learning truths about the world around us, yet not a single person or source who has taught us that truth has been perfect, because perfection isn't necessary to speak or even live out the truth.

Truth is deeper and richer, stronger and more transcendent, than any historical or even scientific account can express. The writers of the Bible understood this. It's why they weren't afraid to use myths to tell the truth about the story of God's people.[3] Myths have the power to transcend time, culture, history, and geography. They have the power to tell deep, abiding truths whose wisdom doesn't require historical or scientific confirmation because that is not where the truth lies.

The truth of myths isn't found in their facts. It's in the wisdom they convey and the lives they inspire. Which is why when we talk about the truth of the Bible or make claims that what the Bible says is true, we need to be thinking of truth in the terms biblical writers most often thought about truth—as wisdom, not simply facts.

Take, for example, the story of Icarus. We all know it well, just as we all know there was no real person named Icarus who made wings and flew too close to the sun only to see the glue holding the wings together melt as he fell to the earth. We all know that story didn't really happen, but the truth it teaches about pride and hubris are just as true as if you could go and visit Icarus's grave today.

That's the power of myth and why myth and truth are not opposites. They're fundamentally intertwined. Truth is not merely a set of facts. Truth is wisdom and knowledge that help us to better understand the world around us and our role in it. The biblical writers—through the inspiration of the Holy Spirit—understood this. It's why inerrancy is not just untrue, it's unnecessary. Because we don't need historically verifiable, scientifically accurate, word-perfect accounts to share and learn truth. We need faithful, godbreathed people to share godbreathed truth. But what does that look like in practice? And what does it even mean to be godbreathed?

Godbreathed is such an evocative image. It's a word that leaps off the page and demands your attention. Ironically, for being such a captivating word, godbreathed only appears once

in the entire Bible, in Paul's second letter to Timothy when he
tells Timothy that Scripture can be trusted and useful because
it is *theopneustos*, or "god-breathed" (2 Timothy 3:16). Curiously, Paul doesn't give any further explanation for this unique
word. It's almost as if he assumes Timothy knows exactly
what he means, so there is no need to pause and explain it.
Unfortunately, two thousand years later the meaning of the
phrase is less clear to us, the modern reader.

That's not to say folks haven't tried to give it a clear and
definitive meaning. Most often, exclusively really, the phrase
has come to be simply a stand-in for "divinely inspired,"
meaning Paul is simply but definitively saying Scripture is
inspired by God. There's not much debate around this basic
definition. The debate comes in when we try to define exactly
what it means for God to have inspired the Bible, how that
inspiration works in practice, and the extent of the authority
that inspiration conjures up. Is that inspiration as flawless as
those who affirm biblical inerrancy insist? Or is the inspiration more organic, a divine push toward the truth, but not a
divine dictation? In other words, the concept of godbreathed
Scripture comes down to a matter of authority, specifically the
authority of Scripture.

On the surface, the matter of divine authority seems to
make sense. In the immediate context of Paul's letter, the idea
is certainly being implied that it is the divine authority of God
Paul invokes to assure Timothy the Scriptures he's been raised
on can indeed be trusted and put to practical use. It is this
foundational idea that inerrantists build upon to erect their
unassailable claims of perfection. After all, if God is involved,
how can something be anything other than perfect? they
ask. And if God is perfect and God inspired the writings of

Scripture, then they must be a perfect reflection of their perfect creator.

More to the point, Scripture *must* be perfect and trustworthy because it is how we know the truth of the gospel, and without that truth how can we be saved? For inerrantists, there isn't just a lot riding on the concept of a perfect Bible. *Everything* is riding on the concept of a perfect Bible. It is literally a matter of life or death, heaven or hell. That is to say, salvation is ultimately dependent on the Bible being perfect, because if salvation is acquired through faith alone, how can one be saved if they have the wrong faith? And how can they know they have the right faith unless all of Scripture is perfect and trustworthy?

The logic of inerrancy makes a certain amount of sense, at least if you don't dig too deep. If right belief is the key to heaven, you need to make sure that what you are being told are the right things to believe are, in fact, the right things to believe. Faith is great, but fundamentalism demands facts, and so belief in facts is baptized and reborn as faith.

But what if faith is more about trust in God than trust in facts? After all, faith isn't knowledge. It's hope, hope that the God who promised to make all things new is in fact in the process of doing just that—breathing new life into the world each and every day. Which raises the question, if God is daily breathing new life into the world, what if the act of Scripture being godbreathed isn't a one-time literary magic trick? What if being godbreathed really isn't a literary mechanism at all, but a life-giving act? And if so, how would that affect or change or disrupt our understanding of biblical authority? Would authority even be the right word to describe the Bible's role in the life of the church?

Consider where else we see God breathing in Scripture. The word or phrase *theopneustos* may not appear anywhere else in the Bible, but the action most certainly does. In the beginning, God takes up a handful of dirt and breathes into it the breath of life (Genesis 2:7). God takes dirt and fills it with the very Spirit of God. It quite literally becomes *inspirare*, the Latin word from which we get the English word *inspired*. Its meaning? To breathe or blow into. No one was around in this earliest moment in history to be intellectually inspired to write, and yet we bear witness to a more dynamic act of godbreathed inspiration than we could ever see on the written page. It's an act of true inspiration, literally a life-giving act that flows from a God whose very nature is love.

Or consider another formative moment in the life of the people of God, this one centuries later on the shores of the Red Sea (Exodus 14). After hundreds of years in bondage and nearly a dozen plagues, the people of God had been liberated from slavery in Egypt only to find themselves standing between the sea on one side and Pharaoh's army on the other. Wherever they looked they could see only death. And then a strange thing occurred. In this moment of hopelessness when all looked lost, God told Moses to turn his face to the water and hold up his staff. There was nothing magical about either the staff or Moses himself. Neither had the power to breathe life or even hope into such a desperate situation. But God did. And that is exactly what God does. The waters of the sea did not divide on their own. God breathed into the waters, tearing them apart so that the people of God could walk across on dry land, away from Pharaoh's army, and toward a new life in the Promised Land.

The same breath that parted the seas once again breathed new life into the world generations later in a rock-cut tomb just outside the walls of Jerusalem (Matthew 28; Mark 16; Luke 24; John 20). There on a stone slab lay the body of a homeless refugee from Nazareth who had recently been cru-cified. A spear through his side had ensured he was dead, an even more hopeless fate than standing between drowning and destruction. But God appeared once more and breathed the Spirit of life into the lungs of Jesus, emptying the tomb not only of Jesus, but of death itself.

Jesus immediately took that life-giving gift and shared it with his disciples by quite literally breathing the Spirit into them—inspiring or in-Spirit-ing them—just as the Spirit had been breathed into him in that cold dark tomb (John 20:22). Pentecost may mark the birth of the church, but before there were tongues of fire on the heads of the disciples, the breath of the Spirit was already flowing through their lungs.

Being godbreathed isn't a mysterious literary method. It's a life-giving act of love that bursts forth from God's very being. God breathes life not just into old books, but into each and every one of us, so that we will be inspired to go and share that breath of life and love with others. This is what it really means to be inspired. This is what it really means to love. After all, that first act of inspiration—of God breathing into dirt—was itself an act of God, pouring the divine love of Father, Son, and Spirit, into the ground to bring forth life. We may not be charged with creating people out of dirt, but we have been charged with proclaiming good news, and the good news of the gospel is that God has breathed and continues to breathe new life into the world. The tomb is empty. Death no lon-ger has the final word. And we have been infilled with the resurrecting power of the Holy Spirit not to control or exert authority over others, but to breathe life and love into people and places and moments where now there is only death.

If this is the meaning of inspiration, of being godbreathed, then the inspiration, the godbreathedness, of scripture isn't about authority or perfection. It's about bringing life into a world of death, which makes sense given the fact that this was Paul's mission as the apostle to the Gentiles, charged with bringing the gospel to every corner of the world (Romans 11:13). The Bible is inspired to inspire us to share that life with the world. That is why we have been filled with the Holy Spirit. Not to keep that gift to ourselves or to perform miraculous signs and wonders like some sort of sanctified carnival sideshow. The Bible is filled with the Spirit to fill us with the Spirit so that we can take that Spirit of life to those people and places and corners of the world that need it the most.

When we misunderstand that calling—when inspiration becomes a source of authority or a justification for oppression, marginalization, and damnation—then we don't just misunderstand a quirky Greek word from two thousand years ago, we transform the Bible into the very opposite of what it was intended to be: into a weapon of death. When Bible verses become weapons we betray the very act of inspiration that gave those verses life. When we transform the Bible into a weapon to be wielded against our enemies, we do more than misunderstand ancient texts. We become agents of death in a world in need of life. Rather than proclaiming life-giving good news, we spread fear and eternal condemnation in the name of God.

It's a fitting parallel, then, that godbreathed Scripture was written by godbreathed people. Because neither of us are perfect. Even in the garden we were never perfect. If we were, we would have been gods from the beginning. But only God is perfect. Even in the story of the so-called fall, there is no description or implication that Adam and Even fell from divine perfection to something less. The fall was from the state of their relationship to their Creator, not in their nature. And yet, like Scripture itself, godbreathed people went on to do great and terrible things in the name of God.

It's almost as if Paul is flashing a big neon sign with his use of *theopneustos* to tell those with ears to hear that the godbreathed Scriptures are written by godbreathed people, which means they may not be perfect. But that's okay, because God doesn't require perfection to carry out God's will. Flawed and tainted with human biases, the godbreathed Scriptures are still useful for teaching, rebuking, correcting, and training in righteousness, because teachers don't have to be perfect to teach. Godbreathed Scripture isn't a proof text for perfection but an acknowledgment that Scripture is inherently imperfect because it's written by godbreathed people. It's an acknowledgment that even imperfect godbreathed people are able to proclaim the truth because perfection is not a precondition for the proclamation of truth, nor is it necessary for loving and serving our neighbors.

The people of God have always known this. It's why in the Jewish tradition inerrancy is not a matter of concern, at least not in the sense it is for Christian fundamentalism. As we have already seen there is certainly an emphasis in Judaism on perfect transcription or copying of the text, but the concern fundamentalists have for literal history is absent. Why? Because the truth of biblical stories is found deeper within, past the literal words on the page and beyond any archeological evidence we could ever hope to discover. Biblical stories are recognized as truth not necessarily because the stories always happened in a verifiably historical way, but because the people of God have seen that truth revealed in their own lives. They've experienced it. They've lived it. It's why inerrancy isn't just unnecessary, it's irrelevant to whether or not the Bible is true.

But biblical inerrancy is not only unnecessary, it is demonstrably untrue in a number of ways, and it is important to understand how and why if we are going to have an intellectually honest faith that doesn't use the Bible simply to prooftext our worldview.

For example, one of the simplest and most obvious errors in Scripture involves authorship. In fact, it's such a clear and obvious problem that while many fundamentalists simply, but intentionally, ignore the scholarship, there are biblical inerrantists who recognize that not every book of the Bible was actually written by the person it claims to be written by.[4] In such instances, they tend to either come up with a clever workaround or dismiss authorship issues as not errors at all, just background noise. But those authorship issues can become quite noisy. For someone coming out of fundamentalism or even still dwelling there, the discovery that Moses didn't actually write the first five books of the Bible can be quite a jolt, one that often leads to more and more questions and eventually the departure from fundamentalism if not from the Christian faith altogether.

Regardless, Moses didn't write the Pentateuch. In fact, scholars are pretty sure no one did.[5] At least in the sense that no one single person wrote Genesis, Exodus, Leviticus, Numbers, and Deuteronomy all by themselves. One theory suggests there could have been at least four sources contributing to and editing together the books we know now.[6] We can catch a pretty clear glimpse of this process at work in the opening chapters of Genesis, where we witness not one, but two accounts of creation side by side, with slightly different orders.

As for the rest of the Old Testament, authorship is mostly based on tradition, although some works like Isaiah do claim authorship. But David almost certainly didn't write the

Psalms. They were likely collected works compiled together by an editor. Solomon didn't write Proverbs, and who knows who wrote the erotic poetry composed in his name.[7] Much of the Old Testament was written during or after long periods of exile, generations after the events being recorded took place. The people who experienced them were long dead. It was the oral tradition of these stories that was eventually collected and written down for posterity. That's not to say the words of the prophets, for example, were invented whole cloth. Many of those words may be exactly what the prophets said or something close to it, written if not during the prophet's lifetime then sometime in their not too distant future. There is simply no way of knowing for sure.

While the New Testament is largely a collection of letters, they are not immune from pseudepigrapha, or texts attributed to someone who is not the actual author. It has long been understood by biblical scholars that none of the disciples whose names are attached to the gospels actually wrote the gospels themselves.[8] It's possible that Luke actually wrote Luke-Acts, as the text itself claims to have been his research project. But it's just as likely that, like the other gospels, someone attached an important name to his gospel because doing so gave the text more authority.

In any case, most of those gospels were written in the middle to late first century CE. Some of those apostles were already dead or martyred. As fishermen, they were likely not even literate to begin with. Paul does seem to have written some of the letters attributed to him, including both those letters where he acknowledges using a scribe and when he makes a point to note he is writing the letter himself (Romans 16:22; Galatians 6:11). But there are other letters attributed to him, such as Ephesians, whose content and style make it extremely difficult to believe he wrote them. The same is true of most of the epistles. They're a mixed bag of authentic authorship and attached authority. Though, at least when it comes to Hebrews, the misattribution of authorship is one of tradition, not text, as the writer of Hebrews never identifies themself.

To be fair, the question of authorship isn't the most crucial aspect of the Bible or the loose thread that unravels claims of inerrancy, though strictly speaking if absolute perfection is your goal, it should. If we are going to claim, as fundamentalism does, that the Bible is absolutely and completely free from any error, then when we discover that the person a book attributes its authorship to is most likely or not possibly the author, even that simple error, while not necessarily undermining the overall message, makes the Bible imperfect. Again, it's a small thing, but these are the sorts of problems you run into when you make over-the-top, impossible claims of absolute, complete, and total perfection. They're just not sustainable, even or perhaps especially in the most simple of matters. On the flip side, if they're not sustainable in the simplest of matters, how is inerrancy to be affirmed with bigger, more glaring problems other than by simply ignoring them or twisting yourself into a wildly complex theological knot that can never be untied?

Running parallel to the problem of authorship is the matter of original manuscripts. We don't have them. Any of them. But you could be forgiven for assuming otherwise thanks to a sneaky trick of fundamentalist rhetoric. When you take a look at a particular church or pastor's definition of inerrancy, as we all like to do when we're bored on the weekend and we've run out of new TikTok videos to watch, you'll notice a phrase that occurs quite often: "in the original manuscripts" or "in the original autographs." What is meant by that clause is a sort of preemptive defense against textual criticism and a tacit acknowledgment that textual transmission and translation inevitably create texts that are, in academic terms, corrupted—meaning there are words spelled incorrectly or out of place, or entire verses missing or entire verses added to a biblical text when compared to another copy of that same time. And not just a few. There are literally hundreds of thousands of variations spread across centuries of copies of biblical texts.[9]

Appealing to the original manuscripts is a clever get-out-of-debate-free card because the original manuscripts—the actual scrolls the biblical writers themselves wrote on—do not exist and haven't existed for millennia. Even the early church fathers who wrote within a generation or two of Jesus and the apostles were relying on copies of copies of the original. Logic would suggest that if you only affirm a text to be inerrant in its original form, then the non-original form that we possess today is not, by fundamentalists' own definition, inerrant.

But there remains the other problem with the original manuscript defense, which we mentioned before: many of the original manuscripts may never have existed at all, particularly the Gospels, at least not in the sort of final form we know them today. Scribal edits notwithstanding, the letters of Paul were, of course, actual letters. They did indeed have an original and complete copy somewhere in history. But in *Gospels before the Book*, Matthew Larsen makes a compelling case that the Gospels were originally less like a book and more like speaking notes—important stories, sayings, and parables that were passed around and eventually collected for preachers to share with their congregation.[10] It's in part why they don't flow smoothly like a normal story would and also a potential reason why stories come in a different order or not at all in the various gospels.

For example, rather than the person who wrote Mark sitting down, creating an outline, and writing out a story like a modern writer might, the writer of Mark was likely more akin to an editor, collecting stories and putting them together as best as he and tradition could recall so that the stories and teachings of Jesus wouldn't be lost when the first generation of disciples went to their eternal reward.

When the other writers of the gospels followed in his footsteps, they too were not creating a new story out of whole cloth. Matthew and Luke in particular drew heavily from Mark's writing, or notes as it were, adding stories they thought were important that Mark had left out and arranging stories differently based on whatever emphasis they believed most important from their tradition's perspective. The same is true with John. As different as the Johannine gospel is from the Synoptics, we can still see this workshop method at work, with John building off established stories, then editing them together and adding sayings or teachings he felt had been left out that needed to be preserved.

When we think about the Gospels, and really the entire Bible, in this way—not as one single book like a modern book is composed or even as a library filled with manuscripts like our concept of books but more like a theological workshop in operation for generations, a spiritual anthology—we can better see and appreciate how the various books of the Bible actually came together as the people of God continued to tell and tinker with and flesh out their story through a chorus of voices. Thought of in this way, we can better appreciate the cacophony of voices at play and begin to see the Bible not as a closed book, but an open-ended storytelling process where even today we continue to tell the story of the people of God, adding our own stories and notes and emphasis as we retell the stories of our ancestors in the faith. That doesn't mean we're writing new books of the Bible, but rather we are finding new, exciting, fresh, and relevant ways to tell the same story the people of God have been telling for thousands of years.

Because that's what they are: stories. They may have some historical basis, some may even be a fairly accurate recounting of what happened in history, but that is not the truth those stories are trying to tell. When people criticize the doctrine of biblical inerrancy, one of the first things they point to are the Bible's scientific and historical inaccuracies. This isn't a coincidence. The Bible is full of them because—and this isn't exactly breaking news—the Bible is not a science textbook or a history book or anything of the sort. But when we force it to become something that it's not, the problems with inerrancy become very apparent very quickly.

The dual accounts of creation in Genesis are perhaps the most notable scientific inaccuracies. But then we have the story of Noah and his ark right after that. Despite some creative math and geometry on the part of folks like Creation Museum founder Ken Ham, two of every creature on Earth simply could not fit inside the ark. But that's only half of Noah's problem, because even if all the ice on earth melted and we had an actual global flood, there simply isn't enough water on the planet to cover Mount Everest under several feet of water.

People have also come up with clever, seemingly scientific explanations for the plagues and the crossing of the Red Sea, and I would be lying if I said I don't watch those shows every time they appear on the History Channel. But it's decidedly much more difficult to make sense of Job or the Psalms writers' understanding of how the world works, at least if you're trying to maintain a literalist position. To be fair, there are biblical inerrantists who recognize the various genres at play throughout Scripture.[11] While they may be inclined to go literal on Genesis and Exodus, they can make space for the poetic flourish of the psalms since they are, well, poetry. Sadly, there are many fundamentalists for whom that is an exegetical bridge too far.

Along with science, there are also a legion of historical problems with Scripture—and not just the stuff way, way back in the past in the Old Testament. The dates and authorities listed by the gospel writers, for example, don't always line up with what we know about the history of the period, which we happen to know a lot about thanks to excellent record-keeping on the part of the Roman Empire. For example, Luke's account of the nativity story tells us about a man named Quirinius who governed Syria when Jesus was born. While there was a historical figure named Quirinius who was governor of Syria, he wasn't governor of Syria when Jesus is thought to have been born.[12] Likewise, if Herod the Great really was king during the nativity, then that also messes up the dating of Jesus' birth.[13] And there is no evidence of a massacre of the innocents or of anyone traveling to their ancestral hometown for a census, a gigantic effort in the ancient world that makes little sense beyond fulfilling a prophecy.[14]

But those historical problems way, way back in the past in the Old Testament are also very real. It shouldn't come as any surprise to you that, despite the claims of obscure pseudo-documentaries on YouTube, even if the story of Noah is grounded in the reality of a major regional flood—and there is reason to believe it may be—there is no archeological evidence for Noah's ark. But while that may not be news to you, you might be surprised to learn that when it comes to the biggest, most pivotal story and figure in the Old Testament, we have zero archeological evidence for Moses or the exodus from Egypt.[15] Joshua and his famous tumbling of the walls of

Jericho? No evidence.[16] Jewish conquest of Canaan as told in the Bible? Not only no evidence, but the evidence we do have suggests the armies and cities listed in the Bible could not have been anywhere near the size they are claimed to be.[17]

And then there's David. The king of kings before his great-great-great-I-don't-actually-know-how-many-greats grandson showed up to become the once and future King of Kings. You know David's story. You know about the giant he slew, the kingdom he established, the husband he had murdered so he could steal his wife, and the elaborate kingdom he established. Like Moses, he is a key figure in the story of the people of God. Not only that, he is a key figure in modern claims by the state of Israel to their ownership of the land that is modern day Israel and Palestine.

You would think we would have abundant evidence for such an important and transformative figure in the history of Israel. We have exactly one pottery shard that reads "house of David" and that's it.[18] That's all the archeological evidence we have that David ever existed. Not just as a king, but as a living, breathing human being and not just a tall tale. Perhaps more evidence will turn up one day. Countless archeologists are on the lookout for it every day in Israel. But as of right now, the archeological evidence or "proof" of many of the key figures and stories we learn about in Sunday school simply doesn't exist. At least not until the time of exile, when, perhaps not coincidentally, the first books of the Hebrew Bible were being written down.

Ironically, if biblical inerrancy has any firm footing to stand on, any legitimate theological point to make, it is here in the arena of historicity. If the Bible is nothing else, it is the story of the people of God and how their relationship with God has unfolded throughout history. While some of those narratives may be myths and would have been understood to be myths by their original writers and audiences, at the core of the biblical story is the belief or assumption that God is actually at work in the world, on this plane of existence. God is not a disconnected deity or a fantasy story in an ancient book. God is active in history. That is, after all, a key reason why the Bible has been and remains so inspiring to so many. It's not just an abstract promise of a far-off esoteric hope for heaven. It's the story of a God who put on flesh and dwelt among us in the here and now. It's the story of a God who gets his hands dirty breathing life into mud and separating waters so people can be free.

A God who doesn't act in history in any way and a people who can't testify to that real, tangible action are not inspiring. If anything, their delusion is quite depressing. Which is, of course, a criticism heard often from atheists and biblical skeptics of all sorts. There is important truth in such a criticism. If our hope is based on lies and fantasies we tell ourselves about the world and our past, then what hope do we really have for the future?

On the contrary, if our story of faith is grounded in reality, in some sort of history even if it's not quite as ready for the silver screen as the Bible sometimes leads us to believe, then we have something more tangible to hold on to: the belief that God will act in present and future, not just because we believe God has promised to act, but because we have seen God act with our "own eyes" in the past. Understood in this way, truth is connected to history, but not confined by it. The stories of faith we tell are true because they mirror what God has done in our own lives, not because they can always be proven by an archeological dig. The most important question then is not "Did it happen historically?" but "Is it true?" Even when we do have archeological evidence for a biblical story, is that what makes it true, or is the truth God is trying to teach us buried deeper?

But the problems with inerrancy are not limited to science or history or authorship. They run much, much deeper, to the fundamental assumptions behind the dogmatic claims. And here is where we come to the crux of the matter. Because biblical errors are not just about getting science or history wrong, or the stray contradictions between gospel accounts, or historically inaccurate stories in the Hebrew Bible. These are the typical areas of focus whenever debating inerrancy. If you were to turn to the many, many manuscripts devoted to defending biblical inerrancy, you would find that the rebuttals to errors pointed out by non-fundamentalist scholars revolve almost exclusively around these sorts of mistakes.[19] Which makes some sense, at least if you're working from the assumption that the book you're holding is a divine product and therefore wouldn't intentionally mislead or teach something harmful. So, if the fundamentalist literature is to be followed, it is assumed that the mistakes or errors scholars point out in the Bible are confined to historical, scientific, grammatical, or continuity errors, each easily fixed with a bit of smoothing around the edges and, when necessary, a hefty dose of mental gymnastics.

To be fair, if you are in that world or if your faith lives adjacent to that neighborhood, some of the inerrancy arguments, if not most of them, seem to resolve these tensions. Or at least ease them in such a way that they can be pushed to the back of the mind, not to be thought about again till judgment day when God can finally explain the unexplainable. Or if not forgotten, they are wiped away through circular reasoning, arguing that the Bible is perfect and true because it says so itself, and here are a bunch of verses from the thing I'm telling you is true that prove it's true.[20] But even without the constant circular reasoning, these generations-long debates about scientific errors and literary contradictions conspicuously avoid discussing the most glaring challenge of the Bible: sometimes the Bible isn't just incorrect about science and history. Sometimes it is deeply immoral in the laws it commands, the actions it condones, and the people it marginalizes.

To be sure, some of those moments are clearly non-prescriptive stories intended to show the reader what not to do. Solomon marrying a small town's worth of women (1 Kings 11:3), for example, is not held up as the biblical ideal for marriage (though it's worth noting it's not exactly strongly condemned either). But what do we do with a God who throws a temper tantrum and drowns almost all of creation (Genesis 6)? Moses murdering someone is frowned upon, but the conquest that followed the exodus was nothing short of God-ordained genocide, at least according to the writers of the Hebrew Bible (Numbers 31:17–18; 1 Samuel 15:3). And those laws Moses said were from God? The weird-to-us, nitpicky stuff gets all the attention, but some of the laws were downright awful, like taking your child outside the camp and stoning them to death if they don't behave (Deuteronomy 21:18–21) or the prohibition against eating bacon (Leviticus 11:7). For all the righteous judgment the prophets called down on the people of God, they also did some rather abhorrent things as well, like Elijah did after he defeated the priests of Baal at Mount Carmel. He didn't take them out for beers afterwards. He had them all violently put to death (1 Kings 18:20–40).

In the New Testament, women and foreigners are repeatedly treated like second class citizens, and as much as we would prefer not to admit it, both the Gospels and the Epistles are filled with anti-Semitic language and sentiments that gave rise to centuries of Christian-led Jewish oppression and murder (Matthew 27:15-26). Then there's the stuff about slavery, too. Paul may not have been a big supporter of the institution, but he or at least the person writing in his name was pretty clear it was right in the Lord for slaves to obey their masters (Ephesians 6:5; Colossians 3:22).

Thankfully this sort of cringeworthy command isn't on every page, but there is a lot of it, and we can't just ignore it or pass it off as the product of a different culture in a different time and place, at least not if we're going to claim that the Bible should still play a central and formative role in our lives today. As we will see, there are ways to handle these passages without ignoring them or doing elaborate mental gymnastics to make them seem okay. Pretending like they are okay or moral simply by virtue of being in the Bible is not only intellectually dishonest and flawed reasoning—it establishes a framework for justifying all sorts of evil in the name of God for the people of God to carry out with sanction and conviction. Not theoretically, either. That's exactly what the church has been doing for two thousand years.

Surely this sanctified oppression and hate is not the sort of thing we must affirm as Christian orthodoxy. And yet at the heart of biblical inerrancy is the belief that biblical inerrancy is fundamental to Christian orthodoxy. To this extent, inerrantists go out of their way to revise Christian history, citing quotes from Reformers and early church fathers alike that seem to support their cause.[21] But the same Luther who we are told said "None of these writers has erred" also called the book of James an epistle of straw and wanted to excise it from the Bible.[22] And the same Augustine whom inerrantists point to for declaring "The Scriptures are indeed perfect" also thought anyone who read the first chapters of Genesis literally was a fool—an absolute nonstarter for most modern-day inerrantists.[23] And as we shall soon see, while the inerrantists are correct that Origen said "The following fact should be understood. The holy apostles, when preaching the faith of Christ, took certain doctrines, those namely which they believed to be necessary ones, and delivered them in the plainest terms to all believers," he also firmly believed the Bible was riddled with mistakes and inaccuracies, or as he called them, "stumbling blocks."[24]

It is certainly possible to find anachronistic quotes from prominent church history figures using words like *perfect* or *perfection* to talk about the Bible long before inerrancy was conceived. But according to their own words and interpretive deeds, whatever they meant by perfection, it clearly wasn't the modern concept of biblical inerrancy.

Yet despite this lack of theological tradition, as well as the lack of any creed or council affirming inerrancy any time before the twentieth century, biblical inerrantists continue to insist that inerrancy is an indisputable and fundamental part of Christian orthodoxy that cannot be questioned. The problem they face, however, is that orthodoxy is not defined by individuals or self-appointed committees in Chicago, no matter how many proof texts they have to prove they're the true guardians of the faith. That's just not how orthodoxy works. Orthodoxy is the idea that there are a set of right and wrong beliefs in the faith—any faith or group really, but our focus here is on Christianity. Orthodoxy has been wielded like a weapon for centuries to damn heretics to hell, but not before literally burning them alive at the stake.

The problem with this approach to orthodoxy—other than justifying murder, which is admittedly a pretty big problem—is that Christian orthodoxy is a very particular, explicit thing. It's not just what you or I believe is true about the Christian faith or what beliefs we think are beyond compromising or questioning and must be affirmed in order to be a true Christian. This means even if we have a Bible verse we think proves our particular belief is orthodox, that doesn't make it orthodoxy. Orthodoxy is limited to the very specific claims made by Christian councils and creeds.

But it's actually more limited even than that, because for it to be truly orthodox those councils and creeds must have been held or written when there was something like one universal church. Not spiritually speaking: the spiritual church has always existed and will continue to exist into eternity. True orthodoxy applies only to the body that proclaims it or decides what their orthodoxy is. This works well enough when there is just one church or at least one mostly agreed upon church authority. I say mostly because as we have already seen, despite the streamlined story of church history most of us know, there were always Christian groups on the periphery who believed most if not all the same things as the "true" church authorities in Rome or Jerusalem or later Constantinople, but for various reasons did not recognize their authority. So even when we talk about ancient Christian orthodoxy, we're still making a generalized statement.

This system worked well enough for a thousand years, or at least as "well enough" as you can imagine when a group of men (always just men) get together and debate over whose ideas will get them to heaven and whose ideas will send them to hell. But, as we have already seen, a curious thing happened in the year of our Lord 1054. Two groups in the one holy united apostolic church couldn't quite agree on the exact nature of the triune God. Granted, the inner life of God is ultimately unknowable, which would lead one to assume that compromises could be made for something no one could prove anyway, but men are often filled with the gift of stubbornness, along with an existential need to win and be proven right. So when it couldn't be agreed whether the Holy Spirit proceeds from the Father and the Son or just from the Son, Christians in the East took their ball and went home to Constantinople to form Eastern Orthodoxy, while Roman Christians said good riddance, we don't need you guys anyway, we've got the pope. Okay, maybe it didn't play out *exactly* that way, but the schism was indeed great, as it has appropriately been named, and the two branches of Christianity—the East based in Constantinople and the West based in Rome—have never reunited since, though there are occasional efforts today at reunification.

Things stayed that way for the next five hundred years or so: two main rival branches of Christianity convinced they were the true guardians of orthodoxy, while Christian groups in places like Egypt, Syria, and Ethiopia were like, "Hey guys, don't forget about us!"

It was then in the sixteenth century that a Catholic monk made more trouble in the church. You know the story: Martin Luther got mad about indulgences—both those sold to free loved ones from purgatory as well as the papacy's overly indulgent love for wealth—nailed a bunch of complaints on a church door, and the rest is history.

What you may not have spent much time thinking about is the fact that with the Protestant Reformation came the formation of yet a new orthodoxy, that of Protestant theology. But this wasn't just a third branch of orthodoxy, it was a splintering of many new orthodoxies, as various new traditions and eventually denominations sprang up in the immediate wake of their Protestant spiritual founder. After the Protestant

Reformation, there weren't three orthodoxies—Catholic, Protestant, and Orthodox—there were several. Even though the Bible was ostensibly clear, Scripture alone wasn't enough to hold the Reformers together. Meanwhile the Christians in Ethiopia were again surely rolling their eyes and shouting, "Guys, we've been Christians for longer than pretty much all of you, for like as long as there has been a thing called Christianity. Could we maybe have a say in this?" But of course, being white Europeans, Protestants and Catholics ignored the rest of the world and focused only on their own internal squabbles as if the fate of Christianity around the world rested solely in their hands.

Luther and his fellow Reformers, whether intentionally or not, tore open the veil of church authority, and there was no going back to the days when people couldn't simply decide on their own that they were right, everyone else was wrong, and go off to form their own denomination with its own orthodoxy. Today there are countless Christian denominations around the world, each with its own form of orthodoxy. The differences may be slight and too nuanced for the outsider to make heads or tails of, but they exist and are existentially important to those who profess those beliefs as orthodoxy. Which they are—in their particular tradition. And that's the rub.

Nothing that comes after the Great Schism of 1054 can be said to be universally orthodox that wasn't already explicitly affirmed by council, creed, or confession by something resembling a unified church. What we have instead are denominational or tradition-based orthodoxies. That doesn't make them necessarily anathema or heresy, and many in each different tradition share most if not all of the orthodox beliefs that were around before 1054. But claiming as orthodox any doctrine that appeared later—such as biblical inerrancy or the rapture—no matter how passionately you believe it or how many proof texts or historical sources you can cite, is not *our* orthodoxy, it's *your* orthodoxy.

So when fundamentalists insist biblical inerrancy is orthodoxy, they're right—it's *their* orthodoxy. But it is not Christian orthodoxy in the universal sense that belief in the crucifixion and resurrection are orthodoxy regardless of denomination because they have been explicitly affirmed in the oldest of creeds, confessions, and church councils.

Again, some will push back and say that inerrancy has always been believed by the church—that the confession of the Chicago Statement in 1978 wasn't a new doctrine, it was simply affirming orthodoxy the church has always believed. Except, once again, orthodoxy doesn't work on assumptions. If it did, there would be no need for creeds or councils or confessions of faith because we would all just assume we knew what was orthodox and what wasn't. But the most assumed elements of Christianity—the life, death, and resurrection of Jesus—were never just taken for granted. They were clearly and demonstratively affirmed in confessions, creeds, and church councils from the very beginning. If the belief in an absolutely error-free Bible—whether in the original manuscript or subsequent copies—was an important, essential, orthodox part of the Christian faith for two thousand years, the church would not have needed to wait until the fundamentalists emerged to tell us that it was. We would have already known so and been confessing it in creeds for centuries.

Biblical inerrancy may be fundamentalist orthodoxy, but it's not Christian orthodoxy.

CUSSIN' FOR JESUS

I started cussing at a very young age. I wasn't brought up to cuss. Swear words weren't a part of my family's vocabulary, at least not that I was aware of. We were holiness people, and holiness people didn't cuss. But kids at school did. Not in class, obviously, but definitely on the playground or whenever teachers weren't around, and they could impress everyone in class with their adult vocabulary. As soon as they did, I followed right along. Not in front of anyone, of course. Even as a first grader I had a holiness reputation to maintain. But as soon as I stepped off the bus and saw it drive far enough away that I knew the bus driver couldn't hear me and rat me out to my mom later, I would scream whatever new cussword I had learned that day at school at the top of my lungs.[1]

I was a weird kid. As I got older, I didn't really get any less weird. I was a good evangelical teenager, which meant cussing was forbidden, or at least reserved for only when I needed to look cool in front of the right people. Instead of actual profanity, I used evangelical profanity. What was evangelical profanity? A laundry list of words that sounded almost like actual profanity, but weren't technically cuss words, so we could feel sure we weren't going to hell for letting unwholesome language come out of our mouths. Words like "heck, "son of a biscuit," "shut the front door," "frickin'" and literally just saying the word "bleep" (as in "What the bleep?") were just a handful of the many entries in our lexicon of evangelical profanity.

You can imagine, then, the feeling of unbridled jubilation I had when I discovered there is genuine, bona fide profanity in the Bible. It's true. Not in our English translations, obviously. That would be too scandalous and profane. But it's there in the original Greek. In his letter to the Philippians, Paul writes, "I regard everything as loss because of the surpassing value of knowing Christ Jesus my Lord. For his sake I have suffered the loss of all things, and I regard them as rubbish, in order that I may gain Christ" (Philippians 3:8). That bit about rubbish? It's a sanitized translation of the Greek word *skubalon*. The unsanitized, more literal translation would be "sh**." I genuinely find "rubbish" a poor translation decision because, in sanitizing the word, we lose just how passionate Paul was about the gospel. Alas, no one asked for my opinion during the translation process.

Regardless of translation or tradition, there is simply no place for the profane in our sacred spaces. Whatever its form, the profane is an unwelcome interloper that defiles the holy, rendering it debased, impure, unworthy, and obscene. As a people called to holiness, to standing apart from the rest of the world as a city on a hill, a light in the darkness, or whatever biblical metaphor you prefer, we Christians try to live out what we believe or at least have been taught to believe is proper behavior by Christians. James warned about the dangers of the tongue and the trouble we often get into with the things we say (James 3:6).

But it's not always profanity that gets our collective knickers in a twist. In fact, there are far more profane things than four-letter words that you're not allowed to say in church, profane things like, "What do you guys think about changing the color of the carpet?" Or "I don't really like potlucks."[2] But few things are more forbidden to say in church than three simple words: "I don't know."

Perhaps that sounds absurd to you, but stop for a moment and think about the last time you heard a pastor or anyone in authority in church—whether your local pastor, a celebrity preacher, or some Christian influence on social media—talking about the Bible or a difficult theological issue and confess publicly that they simply don't know the answer to the challenge at hand. I mean it. Really think about the last time a person in authority at church or the extended Christian world admitted there was some question related to faith or the Bible or Jesus that they didn't know the answer to or didn't have a preplanned answer ready to go that you've heard a million times before.

In the social media age, the need for affirmation and platform growth breeds surety, even among those of us not seeking to become famous. The internet works like a public square where we can share our ideas with others and hear what others think, at least in theory. In reality, it is our chance to prove we're right and everybody else is wrong. Social media breeds an addiction to affirmation for all of us who dare to dip our toes in its chaotic waters.

But in the context of the church this becomes particularly problematic, because we're not just battling over the best sports team or an artist's place on the list of greatest musicians of all time. We're waging a battle over heaven and hell, life and death, and we've been fighting it since long before Al Gore invented the internet. There is no space to be wrong, let alone admit we don't know something, because the consequences are simply too grave. Humility and doubt and questions don't just become a liability, they become sin, an affront to the clarity of Scripture and a threat to the perfectly fortified walls of ortho-doxy. Humility and doubt call into question the boundaries of who's in and who's out and who believes the right thing, and there is nothing more important than having the right beliefs. Eternity and personal reputations depend upon it.

It should be no wonder then to see so many recoil in horror or at least vent their frustration at the wave of deconstruc-tion passing through the church today. It feels like a personal attack, as if those asking questions about their own faith are subliminally criticizing those who don't have doubts. Rather than standing ready with open arms to walk beside our broth-ers and sisters as they share their doubts and struggles and pain, too many in the church shout them down, kick them out, accuse them of maliciously leading others astray, or dismiss them as never having had faith at all. We have saving knowl-edge and vulnerable believers to protect.

So gatekeepers appoint themselves to stand up and speak out, to shut down those who dare to doubt or question, and in doing so lead the faithful to begin to have their own doubts and questions, which could leave to the ultimate calamity: a drop in membership. Though I wonder sometimes if the zeal of the gatekeepers isn't simply an effort to defend the faithful from the wolves, but also a bulwark against having to ask dif-ficult questions about the problematic consequences of their own theology. I wonder if sometimes it's easier to damn others to hell than it is to look in the mirror and ask ourselves hard questions. I wonder if we fear the answers we might find and have decided it's better not to ask them at all.

On the one hand, this makes sense. Gatekeepers and laity alike often have a good thing going in their spiritual lives.

Salvation seems assured. Why threaten that? Then again, if their faith is as rock solid and unassailable as they claim, why feel threatened at all? If you truly believe you have all the answers, shouldn't the doubts and questions of the deconstructing be something to celebrate? A moment to help others in the faith grow in knowledge and understanding? If Christianity and the Bible really are as rock solid and unassailable as fundamentalism claims, shouldn't deconstruction be a normal, welcome, and critical part of growing in faith that refines someone's faith into something even stronger, rather than a wolf in sheep's clothing, a profane interloper sowing doubt and sullying the purity of the holy? In other words, if knowledge or belief is as essential to salvation as some claim, then shouldn't the process of learning, understanding, and even doubting that knowledge not just be critical, but holy and essential?

Good stories should be able to withstand even the most challenging questions. If they're truthful, good stories need not fear questions or doubt or even rejection. Perhaps, then, it is the doubts of the gatekeepers and not the deconstructing that are the true threat. Not to the truth of the story, but to the power, control, and authority of those who tell the story and dictate its meaning.

Regardless of motive, it is in this toxic stew of hubris and pride that things like doubt and questions become sin, profane interlopers in the sanctuary of surety. There are echoes of Eden in this need for perfect knowledge of everything, this need to control the world around us as if we ourselves were the lords of all creation. We snatch at divinity when we should be humbled by the immense complexity around us (Philippians 2:1–7). Rather than admitting our understanding is limited by the dim mirrors through which we see the world, we double down in the sureness that we are right. We must. After all, we've been conditioned to believe that right belief is the key to avoiding hell. When right ideas become the ticket to paradise, the Bible is transformed into an answer book, the answer key to salvation. It must. Without the right answers we face eternal damnation.

And yet when we approach the Bible on its own terms and resist the temptation to transform it into what we need it to be and instead let it breathe and speak on its own, we find a Bible that asks far more questions than it provides answers. *Am I my brother's keeper? Who do you say that I am? My God, my God, why have you forsaken me?*

But we have made our churches enclaves of confidence. In such spaces, answers are holy, and doubt, questions, and even humility become profane, unwelcome, and condemned as a perversion of a perceived holy calling to be right, confident, and in possession of all knowledge. We are but jars of clay and yet have ordained ourselves arbiters of all truth. We see but through a mirror dimly and yet have convinced ourselves we have pierced the veil of the divine and behold the mysteries within with perfect vision. The church may have an ancient apophatic tradition of embracing silence in the face of unknowable divine mysteries, but that tradition has no place in a modern world where right answers are the key to heavenly bliss and earthly power. And so we've transformed the Bible into what we need it to be: the answer key for our salvation. Follow these rules or verses I picked out to emphasize, and follow them the way I see them, or I will damn you to hell for all eternity.

Humility is both the problem we face and its solution. We lack it, but desperately need its liberation from our pride. Humility has become a virtue with little place in the modern world, but if Paul was right when he recited one of church's earliest hymns to the faithful in Philippi, then humility is at the very core of what it means to be Christlike (Philippians 2:6–11). After all, though being in the form of God, Jesus did not try to snatch divinity for himself but rather humbled himself, took on the form of a slave, and died a humiliating death. As we know, that death wasn't the end of the story. Christ's humiliation led to life, not death, and not just for him, but for all creation. It is this sort of life-giving humility Paul challenges us to embody as followers of Jesus, yet too often we treat the way of Jesus and the lessons of the Bible as a competition to prove who is right and who is wrong. Or more to the point, who is going to heaven and who is going to hell.

The hubris we bring to biblical interpretation is all the more striking given what the Bible itself has to say about our ability to fathom the mysteries of the divine. Paul rightly describes the good news of the gospel, but declares its messengers are but jars of clay, earthly vessels that are inherently weak and flawed (2 Corinthians 4:7). It becomes all the more striking of a metaphor when you remember that many of our oldest biblical texts were preserved in literal clay jars, fickle and flawed vessels that shatter to pieces when mishandled. As we've seen repeatedly, Paul also declares that we see the mysteries of God only through a mirror dimly (1 Corinthians 13:12). It's almost as if Paul is screaming out, "Guys, we don't have this all figured out and we won't this side of eternity. It's just not possible. So maybe hold your horses a bit on the whole 'the Bible is clear' stuff."

That's not to say the Bible can't be clear in some places. It can be, but phrases like "the Bible says" or "the Bible is clear" are inherently meaningless and ultimately unhelpful. Why? Because the Bible is not a single, unified book like we think of a book today. It doesn't speak with one voice or one author. It's a collection of books written by dozens of different people across many centuries. It's more akin to a library, a literary workshop, or an anthology. Are there overlapping themes among some of those books? Absolutely. Do many of those books share similar messages and ideas? Of course. But saying "the Bible is clear" or even "the Bible says" is akin to saying "the library is clear" or "the library says" about a given subject.

Rather than trying to force all sixty-six books of the Bible to speak in one accord, it's better—and by better I mean more accurate and intellectually honest—to look at individual books first and try to discern their meaning and the stories they are trying to tell before comparing those stories and themes to other books in the Bible. But even there, the Bible is not always as clear as we would like it to be. From the very beginning, pun very much intended, the book of Genesis gives us multiple, sometimes contradicting accounts of creation (Genesis 1–2). In fact, throughout the Pentateuch—the first five books of the Hebrew Bible—we get multiple accounts of the same event or even the same law, the mark of multiple editors at work making sure the right meaning is told, thereby unintentionally leaving us with multiple right meanings and a text that is often anything but clear or plain.

What about the New Testament? Are there passages within the Gospels whose meaning is plain and clear without the need for deep, complex, academic exegesis? Sure. But even straightforward commandments like "Love your neighbor" leave a whole lot of room for trying to figure out what that practice looks like in real life. Then there are a whole host of seemingly straightforward passages with plain meanings that often get allegorized because the teaching is too hard: like sell everything you have and give it to the poor, or cut off your hand if it causes you to sin. Curiously, there are not many fundamentalists out there demanding a literal reading of Scripture who find themselves living in poverty and missing a hand. As Rachel Held Evans liked to say, everyone's a literalist until the Bible starts talking about gluttony.[3]

Of course, the lack of clarity doesn't stop with the Gospels. Paul is famous for emphasizing that faith alone will save us (Romans 3:28), or at least that's what Luther tells us Paul said. But Paul's contemporary James, the brother of Jesus, was just as emphatic that faith without works is dead because faith alone cannot save us (James 2:24). Then, almost as if it was intended as a long-simmering inside joke about biblical clarity, we get to the book of Revelation. It's meaning is not nearly as impenetrable as it might appear at first glance, but it's also not the clear road map to the future that certain televangelists or fictional book series about the rapture would leave you to believe through the purchase of their many books, study guides, and video series explaining in detail the mysteries that not even John himself seemed to understand.[4]

Now, you might be thinking to yourself, "Self, I already knew this. Obviously the Bible is a massively complex collection of incredibly diverse perspectives written across countless generations. Obviously it's not always plain and clear. How can these folks not see that?" The answer to that lies in one of the key pillars of fundamentalism: authority. You know the line: The Bible says it, I believe it, that settles it. It's a powerfully seductive one-liner that seems to instantly and definitively settle any Bible dispute. In practice, the appeal to higher authority is devastatingly effective in its ability to squash doubt and silence dissent.

We've seen how the circular reasoning of self-referential authority is employed by using Bible verses to prove other

Bible verses and even the perfection of the Bible itself. But there's a more insidious and intellectually dishonest use of authority that serves as a final, shaming, manipulative, and damning trump card against anyone who disagrees with the pastor or internet troll. And that is the idea that the Bible is the final and ultimate authority in the Christian faith. It's a powerful and nice-sounding idea for folks who like to brand themselves as Bible-believing Christians. (As opposed to Christians who don't believe in the Bible?) And it's one with a kernel of historical truth to it.

The Bible has been in the highest echelon of church authority for as long as there has been a Bible. Though it's worth noting that for the fifteen hundred years before Martin Luther invented *sola scriptura*, the Bible was an authority alongside the people who gave it authority—the church—not an autonomous authority all by its lonesome.

The problem—given that the Bible is not a living, breathing, autonomous person, but rather a collection of written works compiled by the people of God—is that it doesn't exist on its own. The Bible did not drop from heaven one day, grow limbs, eyes, and a mouth, and become God incarnated in paper and ink. The Bible only has authority to the extent that we, the people of God, give it authority. Let me say that again: the Bible has no authority outside of the community of faith that gives it authority. That's why your been-to-Sunday-school-every-day-of-his-life Uncle Carl lives according to what *he* believes the Bible says he should do and your nice-but-couldn't-care-less-about-the-Bible neighbor next door spends her mornings gardening instead.

The Bible has authority because we give it authority in our own lives. The books within the Bible have authority because the church chose to give them biblical authority by placing them in the canon rather than other books written around the same time. As we've seen, that process wasn't the nefarious stuff of Dan Brown and *The Da Vinci Code*. Those books were chosen because they already had pragmatic authority in the community of early Christians. They were seen as inspired because they inspired the people of God to better live out the kingdom of God on earth as it is in heaven. And because of that, the people of God chose to include those books as part of their collection of sacred texts. But all along the way—from writing to editing to compiling to canonizing to the creation of Hobby Lobby Bible art—we the people of God have played a fundamental and essential role in the Bible's place of authority in the life of the church.

So when folks talk about being under the authority of Scripture or claim there is no higher authority than the Bible, that is simply not true. It's a deflection to avoid personal accountability. We can certainly choose to follow as rigorously as we like whatever passages of scripture we choose, but we are still inescapably involved in that process. We are choosing to give particular verses authority in our lives just as we choose to believe the Bible as a whole is the primary authority in our lives. But in both cases, the simple fact of the matter is that we, not a book, are the ultimate authority in our relationship to the Bible by choosing to let the Bible have authority in our lives.

It is when we deny this essential element of Biblical authority—when we excise ourselves out of the interpretative process and claim we are simply repeating the unvarnished truth of God, and if you're mad at me for saying so you're really just mad at the Bible—that the holy Scriptures, meant to inspire the people of God to live like the people we've been called to be, are transformed into a weapon. We tell ourselves, we're just repeating what the Bible says. In truth we are no different than Pilate washing our hands of any guilt that comes from our weaponization of the word.

The sort of power and authority that come from claiming you are simply repeating what the Bible says, as if its meaning is so plain and clear that you are playing no interpretative role, is deeply intoxicating for pastors and laity alike. It is as if you are the mouthpiece of God, an empty vessel merely functioning as vocal cords for the voice of God. Should anyone disagree, dispute, or doubt you, they aren't casting aspersions on a mere mortal. They are attacking God. It's a toxic dynamic ripe for abuse in a whole host of ways, turning everyone from fellow believers in the next pew to biblical scholars into enemies of God. From women and minorities, to immigrants and the LGBT community, no one is safe from the wrath of the self-anointed.

This sort of sanctified pride, this holy hubris, is antithetical to the way of Jesus, who rejected the idea of power, control, and manipulating people into following him. But one cannot claim perfection and perfect knowledge from a place of humility. Which is why inerrancy isn't just untrue, it's anti-Christ in the truest sense of the word. Rather than following the way of Jesus, inerrancy chooses the path of Icarus. Full of the confidence that it has figured out the mysteries of the heavens and is but one leap heavenward from taking its eternal reward for its vociferous, take-no-prisoners defense of the faith, inerrancy leaves no space for Christlike humility.

But God doesn't need us to defend God. Or the Bible. Being able to explain why you believe the things you believe is not a bad thing. But in our defensiveness and need to be right, we've turned the Bible into an idol and our opinion into the very words of God. God bound in leather, beyond questioning, doubt, or imperfection. We will defend our theology at all costs until we have no energy or interest left for defending the poor, the lost, the least, or anyone else Christ came to save. In doing so, the Bible is transformed from a source of hope and new life into a list of facts to memorize and a weapon of oppression to wield against our enemies should they question our beliefs or treatment of our neighbors. As a tool of inquisition, rarely inspiring hope in the so-called lost, the Bible's message of good news gets lost in an angry shouting match about sin and vengeance.

Is that why the Bible exists? Is its purpose really to be a weapon of death and damnation to wield against apostates and backsliders? If it is, then why do we even bother reading it or sharing its stories? We claim it is because it is the word of God, but is such a weaponizing of Scripture a meaning worthy of God? Surely not. Surely a gospel of legalism and ostracizing is not worthy of a God who gave birth to creation as an act of love and indeed whose very essence is loving communion. Surely the God who so loved the whole world that God put on flesh, dwelt among the least as the least, and died at the hands of an oppressive empire deserves a book with a better story to tell than "Here are a list of sins, don't do them; say a prayer and believe the right things and God won't torture you in hell for eternity." Surely the story of God is better, more hopeful, more loving, more meaningful than that.

The early church father Origen thought so. You may not be familiar with him, but outside of perhaps Augustine, no early church father has had a greater impact on the shaping of theology in the church. Writing just a handful of generations after Jesus, before there was even such a thing as Christian orthodoxy, let alone an official Bible—just a list of books the people of God had come to recognize as important for understanding their story and what it meant to be followers of Jesus—Origen set out this challenge to the people of the book: we "should try to discover in the Scripture which we believe to be inspired by God a meaning worthy of God."[5]

This is where defenses of the faith, or apologetics, and with it inerrancy, lose their way. So concerned with being right and others being wrong, they lose sight of why the Bible exists at all. Instead of being a word from God that challenges us and inspires us to live out the good news, the Bible is stripped of all its holy meaning, reduced to little more than an answer book to prove others wrong and a legal code to damn them to hell.

At its best, a defense of the faith reveals why Christianity is worth believing in at all. At its best, a defense of the Bible reveals a meaning worthy of the God it proclaims. At its very best, apologetics isn't an argument with nonbelievers, but a way of life, a shining light on a hill that beckons all to come inside and take their seat at the table of God.

If we want to find in Scripture a meaning worthy of God, we will find that meaning by living it out. We can't simply compile a list of proof texts or write a dissertation about why the Bible is worthy of being called godbreathed, just like Jesus couldn't simply stand on a hillside and lecture. We have to put that meaning, that holy breath of God, into action by making it a way of life and not just a list of verses to memorize or memes to create. And we must do it with Christlike humility in all things—including theology—otherwise we are nothing more than clanging gongs making noise no one wants to hear.

The question, of course, is how do we do that? How do we go about finding a meaning worthy of God in Scripture that often has stories that are anything but worthy of God, at least not the sort of loving God worthy of proclaiming good news about? Where is good news to be found in stories of global annihilation, incest, murder, rape, adultery, genocide, misogyny, or slavery?

For many these stories are, understandably enough, reason not to find the Bible worth reading at all. I get that. I really do. If we read the Bible like we read any other book and take everything it says uncritically and prescriptively, the Bible can lead and has led folks to some very dark places in the name of God.

While we can't simply ignore those passages, because for good or ill the entire Bible is our story to tell, we also don't have to fall for the fundamentalist claim that anything other than complete obedience and acceptance of the text (or rather, their interpretation of the text) is sin or heresy or whatever epithet they prefer. Without inerrancy, we are told, biblical interpretation is impossible and arbitrary. Without affirming as absolute truth every word of every sentence in Scripture, we are told, we're just picking and choosing which passages to follow and which to ignore based on our own desires, flippantly with no guide but our gut instinct.

I would like to suggest there is at least one other option out there, a way to read and apply the Bible that is as intellectually honest as it is life-giving. To do that, we have to turn to two guides who have had immeasurable influence on Christian theology, but who would likely be kicked out of many churches today for some of the things they taught and believed about the Bible.

WHAT IF THE BIBLE IS WRONG?

It didn't take me long after arriving at Yale to realize just how in over my head I really was. I had strolled onto campus with my fancy-pants GPA from an earlier graduate program, sure I knew exactly what I was getting into and already with a leg up on the poor ignorant souls who were coming straight from undergrad. That fantasy ended rather abruptly as I found there was an entirely new academic language to learn and a new world of resources to discover and implement that I heretofore had no idea even existed.

Just how much did I embarrass myself? In response to one of my first papers, a paper I was sure would earn an A or at the very least a solid B with high praise, my professor wrote, "You cannot write a paper on the gospel of Mark without consulting my wife's commentary." Now, before you go writing off that professor as an arrogant jerk, let me assure you he was simply stating the truth. His wife is a world-renowned New Testament scholar, a fact I was wholly unaware of. I was also completely unaware that the commentary series she contributed to even existed.

I had my set of resources and experts. I had accumulated them through four years of undergrad and two more years of graduate school at an evangelical university. But what I didn't realize was just how enclosed my evangelical bubble really was. Even though we prided ourselves on being open-minded and well educated, the truth was, there was still so much out there for me to learn, so much I didn't have a clue about.

Pride shattered, it took me a bit to find my feet again and, more importantly, come to accept the fact that just like the undergrads I had smugly looked down on, I still had a lot to learn. But once I got to that point of contrition, a world of possibility began to open up. Despite my less-than-stellar performance the first time around, I signed up for another class with that same professor who wasn't as impressed with my first paper as I had been. You may be wondering why I took a class from a professor I had already so thoroughly embarrassed myself in front of. Some of it had to do with being a glutton for punishment. But the real reason I was in his class was the same reason I had come to Yale in the first place. I wanted to learn from the best of the best, and he is one of the very best New Testament scholars you could ever hope to take a class from. Not just because he is one of the top New Testament scholars in the world, but because he seemed to genuinely enjoy the profession of teaching, something that could not always be said of some of his colleagues. He even regularly ate lunch with students in the commissary, a tragically rare sight in graduate school. Oh, and he has an Irish accent. If you're an American, you know it's scientifically impossible not to be immediately entranced by someone with an Irish accent.

But it was his expertise that drew me into his orbit. He had an encyclopedic knowledge of the material he taught. He could cite verses, sources, and Dead Sea Scrolls like he was reciting his own children's names. But he also listened. He said what needed to be said to start and guide the conversation, but left ample room for students to share their thoughts, opinions, and questions. This time around, I mostly sat silent in his class. Call it shattered pride or cowardice, but I told myself I wanted to really listen and learn, not just from him, but from my fellow students, who came from backgrounds radically different from my own and who, as a result, asked questions that never would have crossed my mind.

We learned a lot in that class, but one day sticks with me more than the rest, in part because, unlike so many other moments in my journey of faith, this is one I can point to precisely. The topic of discussion that day was the messy parts of the Hebrew Bible, in particular the parts of the Law that called on the people of God to do such unbelievable things as take their children outside the camp if they were being too bratty and stone them to death (Deuteronomy 21:18–21). The challenge for us was to figure out a way to deal with such awful commands in light of the fact that, regardless of being in the Bible, they were awful things to tell people to do.

I had my own mental acrobatics that I had learned in Sunday school for dealing with such passages and learned quickly my routine was shared by many others in class. Some suggested the passage didn't matter anymore in light of Jesus. Others argued the people of Israel were simply putting words in God's mouth because there was no way God would say something like that. Some folks pointed to the importance of understanding the radically different historical context. Still others offered more complex rationales that, I admit, I had a hard time following.

The professor listened patiently to everyone's ideas and with each presentation smiled politely with the smile we knew meant "That's cute, but no." Once the class seemed exhausted of ideas and rationales, our professor offered up a question that seems so obvious and simple now, yet rocked my world nonetheless. "What if," he said, "the Bible is simply wrong?" Why, he asked, do we feel compelled to do mental gymnastics to avoid saying the obvious about an injunction we would condemn without question were it to appear anywhere else?

It was like a bomb went off. You could hear a pin drop. Pick your favorite metaphor. But whether conservative or liberal, it was like scales falling off most of our eyes, because whether we still clung to the theology of our youth or not, there was still a mental barrier erected deep in our brains that kept us from acknowledging the obvious: the Bible was written by people and people are sometimes wrong. Not just about small things. Big things, too. Even when we try to tell the truth and try to get it right, we screw up. Constantly. We just can't get out of our own way, and we make mistakes.

But when we talk about mistakes or problems or errors or whatever you want to call them in the Bible, we often focus on things like history, science, or the number of people in one gospel story compared to the number of folks in the same story in a different gospel. The contradictions and inaccuracies have centuries worth of rationalizations written to reconcile the glaring discrepancy with whatever problem the interpretation requires to be smoothed out. It is these moments of inaccurate history, science, and textual issues that most biblical inerrantists work to address, reconcile, or find a way to dismiss as unimportant. Though there are inerrantists out there who insist that no, actually history and science are wrong because the Bible can't be wrong because it's the Bible.[1] There is no arguing or debating with folks like this about how the Bible could be scientifically accurate when it says there was light before the sun, moon, and stars were created. But those who do see the issues and work hard to address them do so in good faith.

The problem, however, is that these matters are not where the most challenging problems or errors or mistakes or whatever you want to call them lie in the Bible. Most folks who don't believe in inerrancy believe the Bible is not inerrant because of the aforementioned issues of history, science, textual transmission, etc. But if we're going to fully rebuild our relationship with the Bible into something more healthy and life-giving, then we must go further still and acknowledge a problematic area of the Bible most of us Bible-believing Christians are still not quite comfortable admitting to have ever considered much. Sometimes the Bible isn't just wrong about science or history or math. Sometimes the stories we read in the Bible are wrong about who we are called to be and what we are called to do.

I know that sounds blasphemous, bizarre, and hard to stomach if you grew up in conservative evangelicalism. It's outright blasphemy to the inerrantist crowd. But how exactly do we call stoning bratty children to death a moral act just because the Bible says to do so? Or keeping your neighbors as slaves? Or committing genocide against an entire nation? We could take the path of fundamentalism and declare that God said to do something, therefore it can't be immoral because God said to do it, but that is extremely poor circular reasoning that creates a very dark and disturbing image of God. There is a much simpler and intellectually honest way to deal with passages like this: just admit the obvious. After all, in any other context would you feel any compulsion to defend filicide, genocide, and slavery as ethical?

Plenty of terrible things that people do in the Bible are relatively easy to wave off as non-prescriptive—that is to say, examples of what people shouldn't do, like when Noah got drunk and tried to go streaking (Genesis 9:20–21). But ostensibly, the stoning of children is a command directly from God, part of the Law that is to be followed obediently and without question. Frustratingly, it is far from the only problematic command or action by God. God saved Noah and his family from the flood, but that flood was a global genocide enacted by God. God liberated the nation of Israel from Egypt, but not without first sending the angel of death to commit mass murder against the firstborn. The children of Israel escaped their Egyptian pursuers because God drowned them all in the Red Sea. When they reached the Promised Land, God told the people of Israel to commit genocide. Even the prophets got up to some nasty things, like when God sent a pack of bears to maul teenagers as punishment for making fun of Elisha for being bald (2 Kings 2:23–24). Actually, you know what? As a bald man, I completely understand and condone that particular act of divine wrath.

Lest we be accused of Marcionism, the New Testament also has plenty of icky morality, too. On not one but two occasions Paul endorses slavery in the name of God (Ephesians 6:5; Colossians 3:22). Then there is his or at least whoever wrote in his name's notorious instructions about women staying silent in the church, again in the name of God (1 Corinthians 14:34). And all of that is just the tip of the iceberg. The Bible has stories and commands from God in it that would be condemned as immoral without hesitation in any other setting. And while theologians great and small have tried to wrestle with these sorts of passages for centuries, too often the wrestling has given way to justification for all sorts of violence in the name of "the Bible says so therefore we must follow it literally and without question."

Consider once again the book of Judges. It goes out of its way to make the point multiple times that, "In those days there was no king in Israel; all the people did what was right in their own eyes" (Judges 17:6; 21:25). It's like flashing red lights alerting the reader to be wary, that much of what they're about to read may claim to be done in the name of God, but folks were doing lots of things in those days in the name of God that were really just what they thought was right in their own eyes. Invoking God merely gave them the permission or at least ease of conscience to do however they saw fit—not unlike what many Christians continue to do today.

Christians of all theological traditions recognize that there are passages in the Bible intended to be followed and passages that were written as examples of how *not* to live. So why not embrace this hermeneutic more fully? For example, when Paul says, "Slaves, obey your earthly masters . . . as you obey Christ" (Ephesians 6:5), why not acknowledge what we already acknowledge about the Bible: that just because the Bible says something doesn't mean we're supposed to do it? Why not acknowledge that the Bible isn't afraid of airing the people of God's dirty laundry? That the Bible doesn't try to hide the stories of the people of God getting it wrong? That, as we see so explicitly in Judges, the Bible doesn't try to cover it up when the people of God put words in the mouth of God?

Can you really make a moral argument for genocide or slavery without a biblical proof text? Some have certainly tried. Slave owners in the American South constantly invoked the words of Paul to force slaves to obey their masters in the name of God, so much so that an entire denomination—the Southern Baptist Convention—was created to defend the institution of slavery as something clearly and plainly ordained by God.[2] Why? Because Paul wrote, "Slaves, obey your earthly masters in everything . . . wholeheartedly, fearing the Lord (Colossians 3:22). But without a healthy dose of "the Bible says it, that settles it" theology, can we really make a moral argument for the institution of slavery?

As I confessed in the first chapter of this book, I grew up genuinely afraid to even put something, anything, on top of my Bible, as if God was standing by waiting to strike me down with lightning if I dishonored God's holy book in such a way. That's not hyperbole. For me, growing up in conservative evangelicalism, the Bible really was a physical representation of God. Even if I didn't articulate it quite that way, it's how I treated the Bible. To even consider rethinking that sort of mentality is no easy feat. To move away from it and begin asking questions about the Bible is an even bigger step. To open yourself to the possibility that the book you once all but worshiped could be deeply flawed, not just historically or scientifically or anthropologically, but morally and ethically wrong in some of the things it prescribes, requires a death of our former selves that can seem as painful as the real thing.

But what if those stumbling blocks in Scripture that embarrass us, those historical inaccuracies, scientific miscalculations, and ethical imperfections, aren't a careless accident? What if they're not something God missed or something God simply couldn't do anything to prevent? What if those stumbling blocks that we do elaborate mental and theological gymnastics to explain away were actually put there or at least allowed to be there by God? Not to trick us or to call what is evil good, but as a way to draw us deeper into the text to the spiritual truth down deep, and along the way to remind us that even when the people of God try to do their best to present in Scripture a meaning worthy of God, sometimes they get it wrong? What if we really do see through a mirror dimly and can't simply quote Bible verses as if they were all eternal laws meant to be followed? As modern, liberal, or even heretical as that might sound, what I'm describing is a way of approaching the Bible that is nearly as old as Christianity itself.

This ancient embrace of biblical imperfection was put forward by an African bishop named Origen. Origen was born in Alexandria, Egypt, in 181 CE. A brilliant theologian, philosopher, and biblical interpreter, he wrote a tremendous number of sermons and exegesis on countless biblical texts, many of which have sadly been lost to time. But his most famous work, *On First Principles*, has survived the ages and is where the idea of Spirit-approved stumbling blocks is to be found.

Origen's brilliance was easily recognized by his contemporaries, even if they didn't always agree with him, and he quickly rose through the ecclesiastical ranks to become a bishop. However, since his appointment as bishop was performed by a bishop from another area rather than his own local bishop, the resulting tension forced Origen to leave his hometown of Alexandria and spend the rest of his life in de facto exile in Caesarea, where the bishop who appointed him lived. Things weren't bad for Origen in Caesarea, however. In fact, life was quite good. With the support of a wealthy supporter and fellow Christian named Ambrosius, Origen was set up with his own workshop where he continued his prolific and inspiring work until his death at the ripe old age of somewhere around 72.[3]

Origen faced many trials and tribulations during his lifetime, including being locked away during the intermittent periods of Christian persecution. He was tortured, but he survived—despite his desire to become a martyr. While he had plenty of theological battles with fellow Christians, he was considered an important teacher in the early church, particularly for his defense of the faith against the claims of the Gnostics. Sadly, several centuries after his death he was deemed a heretic, a declaration now seen by most Christian theologians and historians as an unfair attack and improper lumping together with a group that had adopted his name but had little if anything to do with his actual theology.[4] That's not to say Origen didn't have some beliefs that would now be considered unorthodox, such as his belief in the preexistence of the soul, but it must be remembered that Origen was writing when orthodoxy did not yet exist. He, like the other earliest Christians, was still trying to figure out exactly what it meant that Jesus had come to earth, died, and rose again.

Origen's most lasting theological legacy was his embrace of allegory in biblical interpretation. It's a bit of an ironic legacy, as early on in his career he was very much a biblical literalist. And by "very much" I mean he would have put today's biblical literalists—every single one of them—to shame. Fundamentalists today claim to take the Bible literally, but conspicuously default to allegory when the sayings of Jesus get too tough. You know, like his call to sell everything and give it to the poor, or to gouge out your eye and chop off your hand if they cause you to sin. The young Origen had no such hesitation and castrated himself so as not to be led into sin by that particular part of his body.[5]

Now, I know what you're thinking. Why would you bring up this crazy heretic who mutilated his own genitals as an example of a better way of reading the Bible? Because I want you to understand the man and know just how seriously he took Scripture, and that any accusation he was a freewheeling heretic who never took the Bible literally or seriously and therefore can be dismissed couldn't be further from the truth. He took the Bible more seriously than most others in his day

or since. Though to avoid an anachronism, we must remember the Bible didn't technically exist in his day, as the canon
had not officially been closed. It's also worth noting that while
regret may be too strong a word, the older, more mature, and
less impulsive Origen did not seem to agree with the younger
Origen on the matter of self-surgery. He was young. Cut the
guy a break. Sorry, *cut* was a poor choice of words.

Okay, where were we? Oh right, I was trying to explain
how this guy I'm sure you now think was a crazy heretic was
actually one of the greatest interpreters of the Bible in the
history of the church. No one, not even the fundamentalists
today, took the Bible more seriously than Origen. I would
go so far as to argue they don't take it seriously at all. Not
because they're not performing extreme acts of devotion, but
because they seem more interested in what the Bible can do for
them than what the Bible has to say for itself. Origen, on the
other hand, was deeply fascinated by the mysteries of Scripture, which is how he saw them. There were certainly passages
Origen would acknowledge could be understood fairly easily,
but he would be quick to agree with Paul that we see now
through a mirror dimly.

For Origen, because Scripture was inspired by a God who
could never be fully comprehended, but who nevertheless
trusted people to write the story of God and God's people,
Scripture was an enigma: not an impossible-to-decipher-or-
understand puzzle, but a challenge that required more than
simply reading and memorizing the words on the page. For
Origen, simply sticking with the literal words on the page or
letter of the law was a deadly exercise, if not for the reader then
certainly for those who fell victim to the reader's interpretation
of the literal text on the page. If history has taught us anything,
it's that Origen was right.

For Origen, there had to be more to Scripture. More than just the cold, stark, unbending words on the page. He was convinced the mysteries of the divine were there to be mined, but he also knew that would require work, because what was on the page wasn't always representative of the God he saw embodied in the life and teaching and Jesus. And so Origen proposed that there were two senses to Scripture.[6] There was indeed the literal meaning—that is, the actual words on the page and what they seemed to be saying. Oftentimes the literal words meant exactly what the Spirit wants us to understand.

But for Origen, there was also a deeper, spiritual sense where the real truth of God lies. To get there, to find this deeper, truer meaning, Origen believed the Holy Spirit intentionally allowed the writers of Scripture to include what he called stumbling blocks in their writing. In his magnum opus *On First Principles*, he writes,

> So for that reason divine wisdom took care that certain stumbling-blocks, or interruptions, to the historical meaning should take place, by the introduction into the midst of the narrative of certain impossibilities and incongruities; that in this way the very interruption of the narrative might, as by the interposition of a bolt, present an obstacle to the reader, whereby he might refuse to acknowledge the way which conducts to the ordinary meaning; and being thus excluded and debarred from it, we might be recalled to the beginning of another way, in order that, by entering upon a narrow path, and passing to a loftier and more sublime road, he might lay open the immense breadth of divine wisdom. This, however, must not be unnoted by us, that as the chief object of the Holy Spirit is to preserve the coherence of the spiritual meaning, either in those things which ought

to be done or which have been already performed, if He anywhere finds that those events which, according to the history, took place, can be adapted to a spiritual meaning, He composed a texture of both kinds in one style of narration, always concealing the hidden meaning more deeply; but where the historical narrative could not be made appropriate to the spiritual coherence of the occurrences, He inserted sometimes certain things which either did not take place or could not take place; sometimes also what might happen, but what did not: and He does this at one time in a few words, which, taken in their *bodily* meaning, seem incapable of containing truth, and at another by the insertion of many. And this we find frequently to be the case in the legislative portions, where there are many things manifestly useful among the *bodily* precepts, but a very great number also in which no principle of utility is at all discernible, and sometimes even things which are judged to be impossibilities. Now all this, as we have remarked, was done by the Holy Spirit in order that, seeing those events which lie on the surface can be neither true nor useful, we may be led to the investigation of that truth which is more deeply concealed, and to the ascertaining of a meaning worthy of God in those Scriptures which we believe to be inspired by Him.[7]

Origen didn't believe the Holy Spirit was intentionally trying to mislead or trick anyone. Rather, what he calls stumbling blocks in Scripture are the result of a real, authentic, and trusting relationship between God and those God chose to write the story of the people of God. Those people had their own biases, misjudgments, and cultural contexts that couldn't be magically erased from their theological imagination. So, for

Origen, the Holy Spirit allowed these stumbling blocks, these theological or historical imperfections, into the text to draw us deeper, beyond the literal sense of the words on the page and deeper to the spiritual sense of Scripture where the truth of God is to be found.[8]

Origen knew that the Bible wasn't perfect, and that was okay with him because that wasn't the point of the Bible. The point of Scripture was to tell the story of the people of God and communicate the good news to all of creation. Trained as he was in Greek philosophy, Origen knew that truth doesn't depend on perfect communicators or historical details. Personally flawed Greek philosophers had been teaching truth with stories for centuries, truths still taught in philosophy classes today. Origen understood that imperfect people were perfectly capable of communicating truth, especially when they were filled with the Spirit. After all, like everyone else walking this big blue marble, Origen had parents. Parents who were far from perfect, but still capable of teaching him about the world around him and helping him to grow and mature into a healthy and productive member of society. He had teachers, too. Before he was a theologian of the church, Origen was a philosopher. He learned all the truth philosophy had to offer, and he learned it from imperfect philosophers. Origen had imperfect teachers in his life, but they taught him a valuable lesson that would come to bear on his theology: the Bible doesn't have to be perfect to teach truth.

If anything, the imperfection of the biblical writers seems to speak to a real and dynamic relationship between Creator and creation in which God trusts us with the most important of tasks. Moreover, in seeing the unfiltered story of the people of God, with all their scandals and faults and failings, and knowing those same sorts of people wrote the Bible helps those of

us who follow in their footsteps find ourselves in the stories
of faith, not as the heroes we love to make ourselves out to
be, but as the equally flawed people of God trying but often
failing to be the people of God we have been created to be.

I find an odd sense of comfort and hope in that fact, in
knowing that the great heroes of faith weren't angels or super-
heroes, but normal, everyday, godbreathed people like you
and me. If they can do great things despite their many flaws,
then we can too and—just as importantly—we don't need to
hide the times we stumble in the process, because the biblical
writers never did.

Acknowledging our own flaws, the flaws of the biblical
writers, the unnecessariness of perfection, and the inevitability
of stumbling blocks in Scripture allows us to maintain our
intellectual integrity as we read and interpret the Bible. It
allows us to have our biblical cake and eat it too, because in
acknowledging the imperfections of Scripture we are set free
to admit when the Bible is simply wrong. We no longer have
to continue to bear false witness about things easily disproved.
We can do this and still maintain our belief that the Bible con-
tains the inspired words of God, because inspiration is about
the indwelling of the Spirit in our lives, not literary perfection.

The image of stumbling blocks can be hard to process if
you grew up in conservative Christianity, but if we think of
them less as obstacles and more like the things that dim the
mirror Paul cautioned the early church about, those stumbling
blocks become a challenge to us, the reader. After all, what is a
mirror's most basic function but to reflect back on the person
looking into it? We tend to think of that famous invocation of
"seeing in a mirror dimly" merely as a caution against over-
confidence in our theology, but what if there is more to the
metaphor than that? If reading the Bible is akin to looking in

a dim mirror, then those stumbling blocks Origen cautioned against become an opportunity to ask deeper, harder questions not just about the Bible but ourselves. We are forced to reflect on our own failures, our own limitations, and the times we've put words in the mouth of God that were little more than our own sanctified hate, bigotry, misogyny, and fear.

Stumbling blocks in Scripture are a challenge to us, the reader, to remain humble in our faith. They force us to confront the limitation of our humanity—our godbreathed existence— while also serving as a reminder of our shared humanity, that even the great heroes of faith we read about in the Bible were anything but perfect. It is in those very imperfections that we find a real relationship between creation and Creator and a God who genuinely trusts us to join in the work of making all things new. And in doing so we are reminded that real relationships come with real responsibilities. We have been called not just to tell a good story, but to live it out. And those stumbling blocks, those insights into the imperfections of biblical writers and readers alike, challenge us to love more deeply and extend grace more freely. For if not even the biblical writers have it all figured out, neither do we. The Holy Spirit didn't allow mistakes in Scripture to remain in order to trick us, but to challenge us to do the work required of being the people of God we profess to be.

Of course there will be folks who will vehemently disagree with any notion that the Bible has imperfections, let alone that they would have been placed there by God. Such an insinuation tends to bring people out in droves to explain how not affirming total inerrancy means we are somehow left to our own whims to pick and choose what in the Bible is true and to be followed. The irony, of course, is that all of us— fundamentalists included—pick and choose which parts of

Scripture we follow or emphasize and which parts we may not necessarily ignore, but certainly don't follow closely. Sometimes those ignored passages are in the Old Testament and are dismissed as part of the Law or old covenant and therefore not applicable to Christians. Fair enough, but what about the teachings of Jesus?

Fundamentalists love to invoke Jesus talking about marriage in the context of a question about divorce to make the profoundly dubious claim that Jesus was also implicitly defining marriage by gender, but many of those same fundamentalists aren't so hard and fast about following Jesus' prohibition against divorce in that same passage (Matthew 19:1–12). Or how about those passages where Jesus commands his followers to gouge out their eyes and cut off their hands if they cause them to sin (Matthew 5:30)? Why are those passages to be taken metaphorically? Because it's so extreme it can't be literal? Perhaps, but how does that rationale also get applied to the story of the rich young ruler being told to sell everything he had in order to follow Jesus (Matthew 19:17–27)? He clearly thought Jesus was being literal when he walked away sad, and yet, with nothing in the text to indicate it being so, fundamentalists often dismiss this passage as a metaphorical tale about the things that we value most.

Then there's Paul. Fundamentalists are quick to invoke his words about women teaching in church in order to keep women silent in the church and yet conspicuously ignore the passages in Paul's letters when he names women as leaders of local churches (1 Corinthians 1:11). And then there's that pesky issue of slavery again. Paul was writing a real letter to real people about real slaves. How exactly were his instructions a metaphor? And if they weren't, then why is okay to pick and choose not to support slavery, as Paul commanded?

The truth is, we all pick and choose the passages we follow and believe need to be emphasized. That's in part why there are so many different denominations. We all have different issues or beliefs we believe are important, even essential. None of us pick and choose from the Bible in a vacuum. We're all part of a particular cultural, social, historical, and theological context that shapes how we read and think about the Bible. We all have interpretive guides whether we realize it or not, frameworks that shape our thinking before we ever even pick up a Bible, guidelines already firmly established about what the Bible really says and what is really important and what can be overlooked.

We may not have names for the frameworks we use to read the Bible or even want to admit they exist. Many of us may not even be aware they exist at all, but they are there nevertheless. That's not a bad thing. We all have our inherent biases and particular perspectives, and those perspectives can sometimes be incredibly helpful to the broader church, particularly if we come from an underrepresented background. The challenge is not to try an impossible escape from the unavoidable. The challenge is to recognize those biases, assumptions, and perspectives before we ever pick up the Bible.

If we can do that, we're off to a good start, but we could still use a guide. Origen helps start us off on a healthier relationship with the Bible, but his fellow Egyptian can serve as a guide the rest of the way, offering us not a cheat sheet for picking and choosing which passages of Scripture to follow or ignore, but a rule for reading the Bible that guides us to a meaning worthy of God.

THE BULL STAMP

When you are employed by a conservative evangelical university and are yourself a conservative evangelical, there are certain boundaries of appropriateness you are not allowed to cross, lest you fall into sin, or worse, get fired. One of my biblical theology professors in college found himself in just such a situation and put his exegetical skills to work to create what I have to admit in retrospect was a clever way to encourage students to write a better paper.

He called it the bull stamp. It was a gift from an equally clever student, and we all dreaded seeing it on our paper. Naturally, I got the bull stamp on the very first exegetical paper I ever wrote. To be fair, I'm sure I deserved it. I was in way over my head. Being the massive Sunday school nerd that I was, I was so eager to take religion classes that I took as many AP tests and CLEP exams as possible so that I could effectively skip my freshman year and the general ed classes that came with it and start college academically as a sophomore. That way I could take higher level religion classes right away.

The first class I ever took in college was Biblical Exegesis, held Mondays, Wednesdays, and Fridays at 7:30 a.m., and it was every bit as painful as you might imagine. More

unfortunately for me, the pain quickly turned to embarrassment when the time came to write my first exegesis paper and I
discovered to my horror that skipping class to sleep in and not
paying attention or taking notes when I was in class was not
the recipe for academic success I hoped it would be.

I knew before I even looked at the grade that it probably
wouldn't be great. In my arrogant mind, that meant a B at
worst. Maybe a C if the professor was feeling unjustly cruel.
To be honest, I don't remember the exact grade I got on that
first exegesis paper, but I will never forget seeing the image of
that bull stamp on the page. It featured, as you might have
deduced from the name, the image of a bull and next to it
a quote from Psalm 50:9: "I will accept no bull from your
house." It was a sneaky way for a conservative evangelical
professor at a conservative evangelical university to say "This
is bullsh**." As embarrassed as I was at the time—I didn't
tell anyone about it for years—I have to admit it was both
extremely clever and very effective in forcing me to get my
act together. I rewrote the paper, got a better grade, and by
the end of my time in college, after I had written many more
exegetical papers, that same professor asked to place my last
exegesis paper in the library as a resource for future exegesis
students to reference as an example of how to write a good
exegesis paper.[1]

I wish I could tell you that bull stamp paper was the most
embarrassing thing I wrote in school. I wish I could, but I
can't. That dubious distinction came later in grad school at
the same university, and it was a paper I am still deeply and
sincerely ashamed to admit I wrote.

The class was Christian Ethics, and I was in the midst of
what the youths today call deconstruction. I didn't believe
some of the things I had once believed, but I was still holding

on to a few things from my conservative past. Partly because these sorts of things are a process, not a moment, but I also hated having to admit I was wrong. I may not have believed in the rapture at that point in my faith journey, but the other conservative values I had come to believe were essential to the faith and essential to defend against what some on the right today call the liberal woke mob. So, when told I could write a paper on any aspect of Christian ethics, I chose to write about homosexuality.

In my then-conservative evangelical mind, affirming homosexuality was one of the greatest threats, if not the greatest, facing the church. Well, that and Hillary Clinton. At least that's what I had been told and come to believe, and the Bible seemed to be pretty clear about it, so that settled it for me. Homosexuality was a sin and even though the handful of gay people I was acquaintances with were nice people, I knew they were damned to hell for loving the wrong people. So I set out to prove why I was right and—as I had been taught my entire life—they were lying about choosing to be deviant sinners.

Coming from a Wesleyan tradition, I thought it would be clever to prove my rightness by using what has come to be known as the Wesleyan Quadrilateral. John Wesley himself didn't invent the method or explicitly describe his work in biblical interpretation in such a way. It was a name given to Wesley's four-fold approach to theology by a scholar centuries later.[2] For Wesley, understanding the faith was built on Scripture, tradition, experience, and reason. In my mind, if I could prove homosexuality was wrong based on each of these four avenues of understanding, my argument would be airtight and unassailable.

Hindsight has allowed me to see this as perhaps my last great stand against the erosion of the last vestiges of fundamentalism in my life. If I could prove my dogma to myself empirically, I could hold to those beliefs no matter what later insights I might gain in Scripture, tradition, experience, and reason. This wasn't just about getting a good grade or even proving to others that I was right and they were wrong. This was about salvation itself. After all, believing the right things was what would get me to heaven—*sola fide*! I couldn't afford to be wrong about something as critically important as other people's love lives. So I got to work.

My inquisition began easily enough. I knew the clobber verses in the New Testament, and I wasn't afraid to copy and paste a few laws from the Old Testament for good measure, so I had Scripture covered. Tradition was another easy avenue. I was a member of a conservative evangelical denomination that didn't affirm gay marriage or gay relationships of any kind. Neither did Wesley or the Anglican Church he belonged to. And I wasn't aware of any instance in church history when same-sex relationships were affirmed by the church, so that was another easy few pages to write. So was experience. As a straight cisgender man with few if any gay friends, I clearly had the requisite experience to speak about the validity of same-sex relationships and whether or not they were truly loving and ordained by God. Seeking out a gay Christian to learn about their experience for my paper never even crossed my mind. Why would it? They were either the enemy or the poor souls I was trying to save. They needed to hear from *me* about their experience, not the other way around.

Reason was a bit trickier to figure out, but I decided I had science on my side, or at least so-called natural law. Sure, there may be a few gay penguins out there, but science is clear that two men or two women are not capable of making a baby and making a baby is the whole point of getting married. My reasoning was airtight. So, I handed my paper in proudly, convinced I had settled the debate once and for all and would likely be heralded by Focus on the Family as the next great Christian ethicist of my generation.

I wish I could tell you I got another bull stamp for that paper. Better yet, I wish I could borrow Doc Brown's DeLorean to travel back in time and tell my younger self to pick a different topic. At the very least, I wish I could bury that paper, that story, that former me deep underground where no one would ever know it existed or that I could be filled with such righteous bigotry. I wish I could wash away the shame of my misplaced zeal like a dirty sidewalk after a spring rain. I wish I didn't need to confess my sin so publicly and ask forgiveness so desperately, but I do. I just wanted to speak the truth in love and save their souls from hell. But for all my faith and theology and airtight arguments, I was nothing more than a noisy gong, a clanging cymbal convinced that my arrogance, ignorance, and fear were actually a form of holy love.

It wasn't until my next trip to graduate school that I learned what it really means to love others more than I love my beliefs. That knowledge wasn't acquired in a classroom, but through a friendship. We'll call him John. We met by chance, sitting next to each other at orientation at Yale. We hit it off immediately. He was a bit older than me and a bit more outgoing, but we shared a sense of humor, a love for Jesus, and all the things that come along with being men of a certain age with family at home. Well, almost all the things. He was gay and I am not. I didn't ask him about his sexuality. I wasn't interested either way. It just came out in our get-to-know-you conversation after I told him about my wife and he told me about his husband.

You would be hard-pressed to find a more loving, caring, or compassionate person than John, an Episcopal priest in training. His gregarious personality made everyone feel welcome regardless of background or belief. We shared many meals together in the dining hall and several classes, too. We've lost touch in the years since graduation, but he was a friend whose brief friendship has had a great impact on me like few others in my life. Not because we sat down and had an intellectual debate about the congruity of homosexuality and the Christian faith. In fact, we never talked at all about him being gay. At least not in the sense that conservative evangelical me would have assumed people talked about being gay. It was just a natural part of conversation, catching up on how our spouses were doing or what surprise we were planning for an upcoming birthday or anniversary. John didn't change my mind about homosexuality and the Christian faith through debate. He changed who I was and what I believed simply by being my friend, by extending to me the sort of Christlike love I had failed to ever show anyone like him. Once the scales of my insufferable need to be right had fallen away and the shackles of fundamentalism had finally come loose, I could look at my friend and see him for exactly who he was: a Christian, a kind and generous soul, a loving husband, and a pastor devoted to his congregation.

By the standards of the conservative evangelicalism I grew up in, the authenticity of his faith would never be questioned—as long as no one knew he was gay. But if that was true, if he was Christlike in every way, even in ways I knew I could never be, then what did it really matter who he loved or who he married? It seems so obvious now, but if he could do and say and believe all the things you're supposed to do and say and believe as a Christian and do them with deep, Christlike authenticity, then perhaps being gay wasn't quite the contradiction to Christianity I had been led—and tried to lead others—to believe.

Now, I know what you might be thinking. I let my emotions get the best of me. I was letting my love for my friend blind me to the objective truth of the Bible. But did I? And even if I was being led by love for my friend, is it really so bad to let our emotions influence our faith? Or more to the point, shouldn't love be a guide to our faith rather than just an afterthought or by-product? Jesus seemed to think so.

Though, to be fair, he could get quite emotional. One time he got so mad at a tree for not having a snack ready when he walked by that he cursed the tree and it died (Mark 11:12–21). Another time he was so enraged by the religious leaders of the day he denounced them as snakes and sons of hell (Matthew 12:34; 23:15). And right before his arrest he got so emotional he sweated blood (Luke 22:44). So maybe an emotional guy like Jesus isn't who we should trust on these matters. He didn't offer a helpful rule or guide for reading and interpreting the Bible in such a way that it wouldn't lead you to write condescending papers in grad school condemning neighbors you've never met to hell because their tradition, experience, reason, and understanding of Scripture led them to love people you didn't think they were supposed to love. Isn't that what good Christian leaders are supposed to do?

Perhaps this is a good moment, then, to look to Augustine instead. The early church father had a few ideas about the role of love in biblical interpretation that might be helpful. Like Origen, he was also from Alexandria, Egypt. That two of the greatest theologians in the history of the church were African, yet white Europeans and Americans tend to dominate contemporary theological discourse, should force everyone that looks like me to pause and ask some serious questions. But that is a subject for another book, several books actually, and thankfully they are already being written.[3]

Regardless of whether you were familiar with Origen, it's likely you know the name Augustine—and I promise I won't judge you for how you pronounce it. You're reading this in your head. Pronounce it however you like. No one can hear you.

However you choose to pronounce his name, what is not up for debate is his influence on Western Christianity and Western thought writ large. This Alexandrian bishop was a giant in the early church whose writings and theology have shaped generations of theologians and philosophers up until this very day. You can probably count his theological peers on one hand. But enough praise for Augustine. We came here to learn from him, not to praise him.

Augustine's rule for reading the Bible is fairly simple, at least in theory. It's also completely unoriginal. In fact, you already know it because you just read about it. While his articulation may be a bit more to the point, his rule is not his own. It belonged to one of his predecessors in the faith: that emotional guy named Jesus who claimed that the greatest commandment in Scripture is to love God and neighbor. Jesus even went so far as to claim that how we understand everything else in Scripture depends on keeping these two commandments. It was a radical idea that Paul too supported when he told the church in Galatia, "For the entire law is fulfilled in keeping this one command: 'Love your neighbor as yourself'" (Galatians 5:14).

So when Augustine appeals to love, he isn't coming up with a new idea. He's telling the same story Paul told and Jesus told before him and the Old Testament before them both. Just like Jesus, Augustine taught that no matter how much work you put into your study of a given Bible story or verse, how excellent your exegesis might sound, how insightful your textual work might be, or how many proof texts you might have to back up your conclusion, if your interpretation of the Bible doesn't lead you to love God and your neighbor, then you're wrong. Period. No ifs, ands, or buts about it. Here's how he put it: "So anyone who thinks that he has understood the divine scriptures or any part of them, but cannot by his understanding build up this double love of God and neighbor, has not yet succeeded in understanding them."[4]

This rule for reading and interpreting Scripture is a deceptively simple one. It's easy to read it from our place in the twenty-first century where the idea of love is typically exhausted by feelings and emotions, but the sort of love Augustine is referring to, the sort of love Jesus described and more importantly lived out, isn't just an emotion. It's an act of figuring out how to love people we don't want to love or have been told not to love. This isn't easy, especially when we've been given a laundry list of Bible verses for why we should condemn them instead of love them. But we're not called to love them as yet another religious task to perform. Love like that isn't love at all. It's a crass objectification, a means to an end that we do not because of selfless love but to ensure our place in heaven.

As Augustine said, "To enjoy something is to hold fast to it in love for its own sake."[5] Loving our neighbors is an end in itself, not a religious obligation to check off the list of requirements for heaven. Jesus understood this more than anyone. It's part of the reason why the religious leaders of his day were always eager to trap him with his words. They were infuriated by his reckless love, by the ways he treated people as people instead of pawns in a game of eternal consequences. So they sought to expose him as a false teacher every chance they got.

On one of those occasions, they came to see Jesus to expose his heresy with trick questions about the Law (Matthew 22:15–40). Which makes sense. The Law was the defining feature of the people of Israel's covenantal relationship with God. It shaped quite literally everything in their lives. So when they came to Jesus asking which part of the Law was the most important, they were certainly trying to expose his ignorance as a teacher, or his blasphemy if they got lucky, but they were also asking a deeply pragmatic question.

In effect, they were asking, what is the foundation of the Law? What is the most fundamental part of the Law that we must understand above all else and which guides how we understand and follow everything in the Law? It was a question of identity, of what should fundamentally shape the identity of the people of God. Jesus told them, "'Love the Lord your God with all your heart and with all your soul and with all your mind.' This is the greatest and first commandment. And a second is like it: 'Love your neighbor as yourself.' On these two commandments hang all the Law and the Prophets" (Matthew 22:37–40).

Most of us are familiar with this passage. Now known as the greatest commandment, its importance as a central tenet of Jesus' teaching is almost universally recognized by Christians and non-Christians alike. But that last bit, about all the Law and the Prophets, often gets overlooked because Christians no longer follow the Law anymore and the prophets are too weird to understand unless we believe they're talking about Jesus. But that last little bit is absolutely critical to understanding what Jesus is saying about the role of love in the life of the people of God.

Jesus is not just saying be nice to people. Jesus also isn't saying you just need to have warm fuzzy feelings about God. What Jesus is saying is the same thing Augustine would say a few centuries later. For the people of Israel—Jesus' family, friends and neighbors, and those listening in the audience that day—the Law and the Prophets *were* their Bible. The Law and the Prophets taught them everything they needed to know about living life as the people of God. So when Jesus says all of the Law and the Prophets hangs on the dual command to love God and neighbor, he's not just spouting hippy nonsense. He's saying that everything we think we know about the Bible and what it means to be a faithful follower of God must be understood or interpreted through the lens of love.

In other words, no matter how much work we put into our study of a given passage in the Bible, no matter how excellent our exegesis might sound, how insightful our textual work might be, no matter how many proof texts we might have to back up our conclusion, if our interpretation of the Bible doesn't lead us to love God and our neighbor, then we're wrong. Period. No ifs, ands, or buts about it.

It's a seismic shift in biblical interpretation for many of us. Because in effect what Jesus is saying is it doesn't matter how clear or plain the meaning of a part of the Law or word of the prophets might seem, if our understanding of that law or prophetic word doesn't lead us to love our neighbor, then we're in the wrong. Period. We've missed the whole point of what God was, is, and will continue to do through the Bible. For Jesus, Scripture doesn't exist as a manual for getting yourself to heaven or a weapon to wield against your enemies or a list of facts to memorize. It's a field guide for loving your neighbor, a fount from which to drink in the Spirit. It's the story of how the people of God have gone about doing that, the moments when they've succeeded and even those moments when they fail horribly, which the Bible reveals they did quite a lot. Not unlike us enlightened believers today who have had the gift of the Bible for nearly two thousand years.

That story of loving and failing and trying to love again doesn't end in the book of Revelation. And that's what makes Jesus' command so fundamentally important both for biblical interpretation and Christian living. It must be our guide as we go about reading and trying to understand the Bible. Our love for God must shape our quest to find in the words of God's people a meaning worthy of a God of love. But that worthy meaning cannot stop in our heads or our faith. It has to be lived out in love for neighbor as well. So that no matter how much we might think we understand the Bible and no matter how convinced we might be that the meaning we have derived from it is a meaning worthy of God, if that interpretation doesn't lead us to actually loving our neighbor as we love ourselves and the God who created us both, then our theological systems, proof texts, or even our deepest, most strongly held traditions and beliefs don't matter. If we do not have love as our guide when we read and share the Bible, then we are nothing more than a noisy cymbal or a clanging gong.

So what happens when we actually sit down to read the Bible and let love be our guide? What happens when we combine Augustine's rule for reading the Bible with Origen's belief in stumbling blocks and a deeper sense to Scripture? How would they interpret some of the more problematic passages in Scripture, or those places Origen calls stumbling blocks? By stumbling blocks, we do not necessarily mean verses or passages that might be wrong in a historical or scientific sense, though there is value to be found there as well.

If we accept Origen's invitation to see beyond just the literal words on the page, we find ourselves freed from the prison of intellectually dishonest fundamentalism and free to discover the real meaning of passages like the creation story—namely that God created out of love and is deeply, intimately, and lovingly connected, concerned with, and involved in creation. God isn't divorced from the physical on another plane of reality like a god of humanism or deism. God is fundamentally connected to creation, because—as the authors of Genesis want us to see through their vivid tale—creation isn't a haphazard accident. It's an intentional, life-giving act of love, the first act of divine inspiration, of the breath of God indwelling humanity to bring us to life.

But what about the more challenging passages in Scripture? The ones your Sunday school teacher preferred not to dwell on because things get really awkward when God starts telling people to kill all the men, women, children, and animals until nothing is left alive in the land the Israelites are conquering? More challenging still, what about the so-called clobber verses, used to beat LGBT people over the head till they confess they're sinners doomed to hell (Genesis 19:4–25; Leviticus 18:22; Leviticus 20:13; Romans 1:26–27; 1 Corinthians 6:9–11; 1 Timothy 1:9–10)? And what about slavery in the New Testament? What do we do with that? Or Paul telling women to be silent, or Jesus seemingly commanding his disciples to pack heat in the form of swords (1 Corinthians 14:34; Luke 22:36)? What do we do with those sorts of passages?

A lot of really good work has been done to dismantle the clobber passages used to attack the LGBT community.[6] For example, the age-old pejorative of being a sodomite has been shown through the words of the prophet Ezekiel to be a condemnation of injustice and exclusion, not homosexual relationships (Ezekiel 16:49). Likewise, many biblical scholars have shown the behaviors Paul denounces in the New Testament that have been translated as homosexual in our Bibles today are not equivalent to our modern understanding of same-sex relationships. The sort of behavior Paul condemns is pederasty, an exploitation of youth by older, more powerful men. It's not a loving relationship that is being denounced as sin. How could it be?

But we can build upon that foundation even further to completely dismantle the ability of those passages to clobber anyone once and for all. Not through intricate, groundbreaking linguistic work or exegetical insight, but simply by taking a step back, looking at how these passages are used, and asking whether or not those uses lead us to love God and neighbor as we love ourselves.

For the sake of argument, let's say the six times in the Bible that homosexuality is referred to are all intended to be general condemnations of any non-cisgender heterosexual behavior. If that were the case, how would the Origen/Augustine framework come to bear on these passages? To start, we must begin where our Creator begins: from a place of love. Love isn't just the framework or lens through which we read and interpret the Bible. It is the very thing that brings us to the Bible in the first place. It is our love for God and neighbor that draws us to Scripture, where in turn we learn how to better love and serve our neighbors. By starting from a place of love, we are better situated to recognize stumbling blocks for what they are because we can immediately see in them that we are being drawn away from love.

But love is not just the starting point. It's also the finish line, and that is where Augustine stands waiting to ensure that no matter where our thoughts wander or our studies take us as we seek to understand Scripture, we always end up in a position to better love our neighbor. Regardless of what we may think a particular verse is saying, ostracizing, marginalizing, and damning people to hell who are different than we are is never loving. More to the point, using handpicked

Bible verses—no matter how clear they may seem to some—to damn others cannot be our takeaway from Scripture because it does not lead us to love our neighbor and it certainly doesn't breathe life into anyone or anything.

What Origen and Augustine—by way of Jesus—offer us is the freedom to acknowledge that the biblical writers were writing in a radically different time and cultural context than our own, that though inspired they were writing with their own biases and assumptions about the world. When love is both our guide and our goal, we can say with confidence that even if the biblical writers do condemn homosexuality in some form, we do not have to accept or affirm their condemnation because to do so, given all we know now, would be neither loving nor life-giving.

Of course, getting to that place of embodying a truly loving and Christlike faith requires a lot of us to admit we were wrong about things we were once certain we were right about. Admitting we are wrong is never an easy task, and it becomes particularly difficult when matters of faith and profession are involved. But if we believe the Bible exists to inspire life through the breath of the Spirit at work in its pages and in our reading, then we cannot use it to deal death to others no matter how clear a particular verse may appear to be. Because clarity and simplicity are not the rules for reading and understanding the Bible. Love is our rule, love is our guide, and love is our destination. We cannot claim with any integrity to be loving our neighbor while treating them like second-class citizens doomed to hell for not loving the way we think they should love. And no, it is not loving or life-giving to tell someone they're going to hell if they don't stop loving the way we think they should love. We're not saving their souls, we're damaging our own.

While the Bible may seem clear to some that it condemns homosexuality, it was just as clear to others in its affirmation of slavery. Slavery is a strange thing for anyone to claim the Bible supports, particularly given how central the story of Exodus is for the people of God. From our perch in the twenty-first century it seems so obvious that slavery is evil. Because it is. In fact, that's something people have known for centuries. Even while slavery raged around the United States, there were voices denouncing it for the altogether evil that it was. Sadly, the opposite is also true. There were obviously many who approved of slavery. Sadder still, many of those voices came from the church itself.

I wish I could tell you the slaveholders were making up their proof texts out of thin air. I wish I could tell you the Bible doesn't say the things about slavery that slaveholders claimed it said. I wish I could, but while the Bible may not explicitly endorse slavery, at the very least it never condemns slavery. Nowhere does it denounce slavery as an institution. The catch, of course, is that the abolitionists were also right. The Bible also speaks of freedom and equality, of all people regardless of race being made in the image of God. As my former professor once observed about issues like this, it's not that the Bible clearly condemns something like slavery, but it does give us the language to do so.

But we don't have to stop with prooftexting. If there is anywhere that the application of Origen's freedom to disagree and Augustine's rule of love is clearest and easiest to apply, it may be here. Clearly, support—no matter how tepid—for slavery is an abomination, a stumbling block if ever there was one. Unfortunately, we can't simply ignore those passages or pretend they don't exist, as much as we might like to. They are part of our story whether we want them to be or not.

But we also don't need to do complicated historical analysis about Roman slavery versus chattel slavery, as if some forms of slavery weren't really that bad, in order to give Paul or any of the other biblical writers a pass. We can say unequivocally, righteously, and without wavering that whenever the biblical writers imply slavery is okay, they are wrong. Period. No ifs, ands, or buts about it. Slavery is wrong no matter how much lipstick you slap on your pig of an argument. We can say the biblical writers are wrong with confidence because there is no way to read those literal words of Paul as anything other than a stumbling block that not only doesn't lead us to love our neighbor and their Creator, it actively harms them, and in attacking God's good creation, we attack God himself. Slavery is not life-giving, it's life destroying. There is no love in oppression of others; therefore there is no God in the institution of slavery. It is altogether evil, utterly unredeemable, and should be denounced without hesitation. Of course, slavery and homosexuality are not the only problematic passages in Scripture. There is also the latent and explicit misogyny that runs throughout the pages of the Bible, perhaps most notably the way the church has used the words of Paul in the New Testament to treat women as second-class citizens in the church. Consider Paul's words on women being silent in the church (1 Corinthians 14:34). His admonition seems pretty straightforward and there are plenty of traditions—Protestant, Catholic, and Orthodox—that have barred women from being pastors or priests because of a perceived prohibition or because Jesus supposedly only had male disciples. While some evangelical traditions have made a point of ordaining women since their founding, many more denominations unfortunately still erupt in uncontrollable rage if a woman even sets foot on the platform in the sanctuary.

But it sure doesn't seem like taking one or two passages from the New Testament, stripping them of all context, and using them to silence women is a very loving thing to do. If, on the other hand, we listen to Origen and see these passages as stumbling blocks to draw us deeper into the text, we begin to see something interesting at work. Not a secret opposite meaning or a proscriptive calling, but rather something we see all throughout the Bible: the people of God getting it wrong and bringing death where there should be life.

There's a significant chance that Paul didn't actually write the words ascribed to him. After all, such an exclusion of women doesn't line up with what we do know he most likely wrote or the sort of radically inclusive ministry the apostle to the Gentiles was committed to. Perhaps what we are seeing in these passages is not a rule for church leadership, but a reminder that the ways of the world that we hear so much about from concerned Christians can sometimes find their way into the church where we sanctify them in the name of God. But marginalizing people is never the way of God. Which is why we can confidently say that when it comes to women, Paul was simply wrong. Because he has to be. Because there is nothing loving or Christlike about marginalizing others simply based on their genitals.

Of course, homosexuality, slavery, and women in the church are but a few of the problematic proof texts in the Bible. There are entire chapters in the Old Testament used to condone violence and even genocide (Numbers 31; 1 Samuel 15). I wouldn't blame you for wondering how those terrible passages ever made it into the Bible in the first place. To answer that question, we have to go deeper into the text, beyond the literal words on the page to find a meaning worthy of God. And when we do, you know what we discover? Sin. There is no hidden special message that makes these passages okay. We are looking in a mirror at our own fallenness. These are the words of fallen people just like you and me, with fallen ideas in a fallen world. That in no way excuses what they wrote. It's sin. The same sort of sin is recorded all throughout the Bible when the people of God failed to live out their calling. The Bible is a collection of stories about the people of God and sometimes those people do and say terrible things—just like us. And yet so often, unlike us, the Bible doesn't try to hide it.

While this can be a disorienting thought when we've been conditioned to think of the Bible as a book of inspiring children's stories or "basic instructions before leaving Earth," it's much more authentic to the reality of the human condition. And it is much more honest about the failings of the people of God than we are today, when image and brand need protecting at all costs, even if abuse, sexual assault, or other crimes are involved. We've convinced ourselves that if we let our sins show, if the outside world doesn't see the perfect image of a sinless people, then no one will fill our pews or want anything to do with Jesus. And yet the Bible seems to be saying the opposite. That it is fundamental to the identity of the people of God—to air our dirty laundry, to be transparent and honest even when we screw things up and especially when we screw things up in the name of God. We are certainly called to be like the light of the world or a city on a hill, but lights sometimes flicker and cities sometimes collapse.

And that's okay.

Because that's the story of the people of God, and because flickering lights and failed cities is not how the story of the people of God ends.

If you've come this far and your takeaway is, "It doesn't matter what the Bible says, I can believe and do whatever I want and call it Christianity or the way of Jesus," I would strongly encourage you to go back and reread this chapter. This invocation of Origen and Augustine by way of Jesus isn't a get-out-of-wrestling-with-the-Bible-free card. Nor is it a free pass to create a new form of Christianity in your own image. This is about taking the Bible seriously. *Truly* seriously. Not as a textbook to be studied, a legal code to be wielded against our enemies, or simply a source of sappy quotes to put on pillows and wall art to make ourselves feel good about ourselves. This is about meeting the Bible on its own terms, about being honest about what it is, what it does, what it doesn't do, who wrote it, their failings and biases, and ultimately what we are supposed to do with this sacred text that for good or ill stands at the very center of the Christian faith.

There may have been a Christianity before the Bible, but there is no Christianity without the Bible today. That's not a defense of legalism or even orthodoxy, but rather an acknowledgment of what the Bible actually is: our story. You, me, your saintly grandmother, Martin Luther, Rahab, Paul, Moses, Ruth, it's our story. We're a part of it because it's a story that continues to be told. Because it continues to be told, we can't simply toss out the chapters we don't like or agree with. That doesn't mean we have to force ourselves to agree with them, but we do have to confront them and try to understand why they are a part of the story and what it is we can glean from them in order to better go about being the people of God in and for the world.

This love-centered approach to the Bible is not only the ancient practice of the church, it is the very command of Jesus himself. Everything in Scripture, and in fact everything we do and say in the church, from confessions of faith to ecumenical creeds, must be understood, interpreted, and implemented in the context and for the goal of loving God and neighbor. This is what "all the Law and the Prophets" looks like for us today. Any deviation from that pursuit of love is wrong. No matter how strong we might think our theology to be, or how long our list of biblical proof texts might be, or how strongly we feel tradition supports our position, we are wrong if we are not being led to love.

Jesus understood the tremendous yolk of tradition, dogma, and proof texts on the people of God. He also understood the centrality of love. It was why he put on flesh and dwelt among us and why he gave himself up to death on a cross. It's also why, when forced to choose between legalism and love, Jesus always chose love. That is the root of those moments that come so often in the Gospels when Jesus says, "You have heard it said . . . but I say" (Matthew 5). Jesus wasn't writing a new law. He was incarnating the love of God. This is why he clashed so often with the religious authorities of his day. They had rules, tradition, and dogma to protect. These were their source of power and privilege, their means of control over the people they were meant to serve.

But Jesus chose to make love both the center and the driving force of his life, so much so that even if the Law and Prophets seem to prohibit something like healing on the sabbath, he had to go in a different direction (Mark 3:1–6), because not healing someone on the sabbath was not loving. The same is true for the Bible. The Bible was created for humans, not humans for the Bible. It was created to inspire and guide us, not shackle us to the ever-changing interpretations of whoever is in charge.

Jesus understood this. Everything he did and taught, up to and including his death and resurrection, were driven by the desire to love fully. He was the Word and the Word was godbreathed. Not the pages in a book, but a life filled with the Spirit of life and love that poured out of that life and love into the lives of others, inspiring, filling them with that same Spirit to go out into the world and do likewise.

That's why the Bible exists at all. Its truth is not found in history and science, nor is that why it was cherished by the early church to begin with. The early church cherished Scripture because they saw the truth of the stories it told played out in their own lives. They may not have been around to see arks float, seas divide, or tombs emptied, but they had experienced God's salvation, God's protection, God's provision, God's life-giving breath in their own lives. The Bible was true for the early church not just because of what it said, but because of the life and love it engendered.

That's where the truth of the Bible is found. That's where a meaning worthy of God is to be found. In love. In a life worth living. In communal, sacrificial, never-ending love for others. That's what makes the Bible godbreathed. It is filled with the breath of life so that as we read its pages that breath of life is poured into us much the same way Jesus breathed the Spirit into his disciples on that first Easter morning.

8

CAN THESE
BONES LIVE?

E zekiel was a weird dude. I think that's why I like him so much. I was a weird kid growing up, if that isn't apparent already. But that's okay. Most of the prophets were odd ducks, too. Hosea married a prostitute as part of a sermon illustration. Jonah took a vacation inside the belly of a big fish. And Ezekiel, well, you know that frozen flourless bread they sell at the grocery store that claims to be following a recipe from Ezekiel 4:9? It's true they do source their ingredients for the bread from a verse in Ezekiel. What they don't mention is the cooking process Ezekiel used to cook the bread: he baked it over a fire created with his own feces (Ezekiel 4:9–12). Like I said, weird dude.

It shouldn't be surprising, then, to find Ezekiel in some strange situations. Like the time he may or may not have witnessed a UFO (Ezekiel 1:4–28). Which, I know sounds crazy, and it probably wasn't aliens, but go read the text for yourself. It was definitely aliens. Or maybe just a weird vision—either way, it's weird. Then there was the time he lay on his side for an entire year and then turned over and lay on the other side for another month, because reasons (Ezekiel 4:4–6). All wonderfully weird stories, but I'm interested in another of Ezekiel's strange adventures: his time in the boneyard. Or "bone valley," if you want to be more specific.

One day, God called Ezekiel out to a valley to show him something God wanted him to see (Ezekiel 37:1–10). The Bible doesn't exactly say that God showed up and said, "Hey Ezekiel, you wanna see a dead body?" but there are definitely those vibes going on. According to the thirty-seventh chapter of Ezekiel, the prophet was led by God to a valley filled with bones. I know the question of how the bones arrived in the valley is maybe beside the point, but I still wonder about it. Perhaps there was a great battle fought in the valley long ago and without enough survivors left to bury the bodies, the fallen lingered where they fell. Or maybe God was just repurposing an old movie set from *The Lord of the Rings*. I don't know. However the bones got there, whether through war or the simple necessity of the vision God wanted to show Ezekiel, the prophet found himself smack dab in a truly bizarre and creepy scene: a valley full of dried out human bones.

It was a field full of body parts with no bodies, no tissue, no muscle, no skin. No chance of doing anything but bleaching in the sun. But if Ezekiel thought he was going to be a bystander in this valley of the macabre, he was deeply mistaken. God didn't allow Ezekiel to simply stand at a distance and gaze upon the bones from afar. God led Ezekiel through the valley on a tour of the dry bones. They walked back and forth together among the bones, almost as if to emphasize how lifeless the bones really were. I can't help but imagine God and Ezekiel stopping at various points to ponder how the bones got there and how long they had been there. And I imagine Ezekiel wondering what in the world was going on.

Then God stopped, turned to Ezekiel, and asked what must have seemed to Ezekiel like the most absurd question imaginable in that situation: "Mortal, can these bones live?" (Ezekiel 37:3) By addressing Ezekiel as "mortal," it's almost as if God was gently teasing Ezekiel, reminding him that Ezekiel may be alive in that moment but only one of them would find their bones in that valley one day. It's hard also not to hear an echo here of God's conversation with Job, when God asks him where the winds and rain come from (Job 38).

God knew the answer to the questions God was asking. Ezekiel might have. It's not entirely clear from his response. We're not there to hear the tone of his voice or see the expression on his face when he replied, "Lord, you alone know." He was right, of course. But it's easy to hear in Ezekiel's response a hint of our own skepticism. In theory, we say God can do anything, but how exactly do dry bones actually come back to life?

Undeterred by the doubts of mortals, God told Ezekiel to prophesy to or command the bones, "'Dry bones, hear the word of the LORD! This is what the Sovereign LORD says to these bones: I will make breath enter you, and you will come to life. I will attach tendons to you and make flesh come upon you and cover you with skin; I will put breath in you, and you will come to life. Then you will know that I am the LORD'" (Ezekiel 37:4–6 NIV). So Ezekiel did as instructed. And then he heard a rattling sound.

The text doesn't tell us where the sound was coming from. It may have been the sound of the bones waking up from their protracted slumber, preparing to be born again. Or perhaps it was the quaking of the earth, freeing itself from its centuries-long burden of death. Regardless of what caused the sound, what happened next must have left Ezekiel at a loss for words.

Femurs and tibias found each other again. Spines rebuilt themselves as skulls retook their places on top of bodies. Arm bones
and finger bones and toe bones all began to snap back together.
Then ligaments appeared to tie the bones together. Then muscles began to grow. Then skin to cover the muscles. And before
Ezekiel had time to wrap his mind around what he was witnessing, an army of lifeless bodies stood before him. But they
were just that: lifeless. So God gave Ezekiel another command:
"Then he said to me, 'Prophesy to the breath, prophesy, mortal, and say to the breath: Thus says the Lord GOD: Come
from the four winds, O breath, and breathe upon these slain,
that they may live.'" (Ezekiel 37:9). The bodies may have been
fully formed but they were not alive. They were still in need of
the breath of life to animate their limbs.

At least two things are particularly curious in this moment.
The first is that the Hebrew word *ruach* translated here as
breath or *spirit* is the same Hebrew word used to describe the
breath or spirit God blew into a pile of dirt in Genesis 2 to
create mankind.[1] It is not just the wind or air or oxygen that
brings these bodies to life, but the very *ruach* or Spirit of God
that brings them back from the dead. It's the Holy Spirit at
work bringing resurrection power to bear on a hopeless scene.
It's the sort of thing we expect the Holy Spirit to do, but what
we don't typically expect is the other interesting thing going
on here.

If the Spirit that breathes new lives into the valley of dry
bones or now lifeless bodies is indeed the Spirit of God, then
God is telling Ezekiel to tell or order God what to do. Obviously that's more than a bit of a metaphysical brain twister, but
it also speaks powerfully to God's desire to include humanity
in the process of its own rebirth, much like God trusted us
to write down the story of redemption. God isn't just saying

magic words while Ezekiel stands by and watches God act. Ezekiel is at the very heart of the action, helping to direct the new creation—not as God's equal, but as God's agent of grace and new life in the midst of a dead and dying world. None of what happens in the valley of dry bones is possible without God, and yet God *chooses* to make Ezekiel an essential part of that moment of resurrection, the vessel through which God's love is poured out into the valley of death—just like God did when trusting us with recording the good news of the gospel. It is yet another reminder that being godbreathed isn't a literary magic trick. It's a life-giving act of love.

It doesn't take a prophet to discern the meaning of this vision. The dry bones represent Israel. At the time, Israel was in exile, taken from their homeland and forced to live under the yoke of a foreign oppressor. Hope seemed beyond imagining. Hope was dead and had been for a long time, long enough to dry out like bones withering away under the desert sun. The idea that those bones could live again, that the people of Israel could live again in their homeland or even just not under the yoke of oppression, seemed as absurd as dry bones magically putting on flesh and coming back to life. And yet they did.

That's the easy and obvious takeaway here. The dead bones represent the people of God in need of a resurrection. Don't hear me wrong. That takeaway isn't wrong. It's easy for a reason. It's obviously right. American Christianity in particular isn't just dying. It's already dead. A recent Pew Research survey predicted that within a couple of decades Christians will be a minority in the United States.[2]

That would certainly make it sound like death is decades away, but when I say American Christianity isn't dying, it's already dead, I'm not talking about how full the pews are. I'm talking about the faith itself, how it's practiced and proclaimed, and whether or not it could be said to be alive by any measure beyond attendance records. Who exactly is standing outside our churches clamoring to be let in? Who is looking in from without and seeing or hearing anything that could be called good news? Too often all they hear is hate and anger and fear and all they see is discrimination and judgment and exclusion. We may still have warm bodies in the pews, but if there's no one being added to the flock, then the flock is already dead whether we realize it or not.

Even if you believe the church is not yet dead, any frank and honest discussion of Christianity in America today has to acknowledge that the church is not in a good place. Maybe where you are, your individual church where you attend every Sunday, is doing well. Perhaps it's even thriving. But this is not the case for more corners of Christianity in America today. The church, at least the church in the United States, is in desperate need of resurrection. The "nones," people with no religious affiliation, are on the rise, and the church in the United States is giving people little reason to want to darken her doors on a Sunday morning.[3]

Chances are you're thinking to yourself, "Not my church!" And maybe not. Maybe your church is flourishing. Maybe numbers are rising, disciples are being formed, communities are being served, and diversity is your calling card. But when folks outside the church think about the church or hear about the church or even just drive by a church, the noise coming from the rest of American Christianity drowns everything else out. It's simply too loud, too abrasive, too off-putting for any of the good things that may genuinely be happening inside our churches to break through and be heard above the noise, the clanging of the gong, the rattling of the bones. Given our inclination to abuse, exploit, cover-up, and enable of the worst tendencies of powerful men, if the dry bones represent the church in America, then perhaps the question isn't "Can these bones live," but should they? Given all the damage and pain we've caused in the name of Jesus, should the church in America even be given a second chance? The answer to that, of course, is in God's hands.

Regardless of how God chooses to answer that question, what if we think about the dry bones representing something more? What if they could represent something sacred made profane, something once alive but now dead, something in need of a miracle? What if the dry bones were the Bible? Desiccated and left to a dry death. What if we are the sinews and muscle? What if the bones actually need us to move? What if, even with our muscles and biblical bones, the body still needs a breath from God? What if the body, bones and all, are in need of a miracle, nothing short of resurrection?

I would argue that is exactly where we find ourselves today. We could rattle off a list of problems in the church: racism, xenophobia, misogyny, hate, abuse, etc. But how many of those things are symptoms of an even deeper problem? A problem rooted in idolatry, in our love for self, and the way we use that love of self to abuse Scripture for our own ends, to wield its power and control over others. I'm not saying the Bible is necessarily to blame for these sorts of things. I'm saying *we are*, specifically in how we use the Bible to justify these sorts of things. Being godbreathed people means having the humility of not knowing and in that humility not elevating our own ideas and assumptions to the realm of the divine, and yet that is exactly what we have done in our idolatry of the Bible and our interpretation of its holy pages.

Nothing short of a miracle, nothing short of the absolutely impossible—bodily resurrection—has any hope of reviving the church from the pit of decay it has dug for itself. The Bible isn't a magic solution to this sort of resurrection. There is no spell to cast or special prayer within its pages that will allow us to skip the hard work of repentance and reconciliation. But if the Bible is as important, as fundamental, to the Christian life as we claim it is, then we have to begin our penance and the path to resurrection by dealing with our dry bones and how they got left out in the valley to rot in the first place.

Because the Bible is nothing, does nothing, can be nothing on its own. God can breathe into its pages, but we are the ones that decide how to move muscle and bone. We decide whether that gift is going to be used for good or ill, to breathe life into the world or to snuff it out. To be godbreathed people with a godbreathed book isn't just a miracle; it's a responsibility to live out our calling, to prophesy to the wind and proclaim good news.

We can prooftext ourselves till we're blue in the face, create linguistic breakdowns of the original Greek that amaze experts, and believe whatever we want to believe about the plain meaning of the Bible with the most passionate of faith. But if we are not allowing the Bible to lead us to find new and creative ways to love our neighbors each and every day, then we are wrong. Period. We've lost the plot and with it everything holding the bones together. When we transform the Bible into a weapon of war against our enemies, in the end they're not the only ones to suffer our wrath. We die, too, as we're consumed by our sanctified hate and fear of the other. Our souls are left to rot underneath the sun until there is nothing left but dry bones with no place, no use, and no welcome in the world.

So if you find yourself wondering if the Bible, like American Christianity, is even worth saving, worth reading, worth centering in the life of the church given how often and how easily it has been used as a source of death and destruction—I get that. I really do. And if that death and destruction have been brought to your doorstep by people claiming to proclaim the plain, unfiltered message of Scripture, I don't blame you for never wanting to pick up a Bible again.

But for all the wrath that has poured from its pages in the name of Jesus, I believe there are dry bones in those sixty-six books worth breathing new life into. Because, ultimately, the Bible is what we make of it. It can be a weapon to wield against our enemies or it can be a story of hope and liberation. A story of creation born out of love, of protection in the midst of chaos, of promises kept and freedom from oppression. It's a tale of obscure and ostracized nobodies taking center stage in God's ongoing work of redemption. It's a place to turn when we grieve as well as when we celebrate, a source of wisdom and prayer when words fail us. It's a source of hope in exile and a call to justice for the oppressed. It's good news for the poor: an invitation to sit and feast at God's holy table. It's a blueprint for radically inclusive community on earth as it is in heaven. And it's the promise that one day every tear will be wiped away. Death will be at an end, and there will be no more mourning or crying or pain, for the old order of things will have passed away and all things will be made new.

When I hear God ask Ezekiel if these bones can live, I hear an echo, or rather a foreshadowing, of the question Rev. Fosdick would ask millennia later: Shall the fundamentalists win? They may not seem related, but I would argue they are essentially asking the same question: What will our story be? Will it be one of life or one of death? As we've already seen and you are no doubt keenly aware, the state of the church in the United States today is not great, to put it kindly. We are little different than a pile of dead bones with little if any good news to offer anyone. When Christians are taking the side of racists and bigots, what other description is there of the church than a rotting carcass?

Fosdick had this same fear a century before our time. He rightly saw fundamentalism for what it is: death. Not always physical death, though the racism and bigotry it has historical supported certainly are responsible for untold numbers of physical deaths at the hands of the people of God who are convinced they are attacking the enemy rather than their fellow bearer of the image of God. But fundamentalism guarantees spiritual death because at its heart fundamentalism is the idolatry of ideas—love of dogma rather than love for neighbor—and idolatry always leads to death.

This is why the answer to Fosdick's question has sadly been yes. The fundamentalists did win. American Christianity is all but dead. It has become inescapably intertwined with the rot of fundamentalism and the hate it sanctifies in the name of deeply held religious beliefs. While there may be glimmers of light left inside, to the outsider, the church is no shining city on a hill today. It's a valley of dry bones, a putrid pile of death and damnation that no one looking in wants anything to do with. It shouldn't be any surprise, then, to see so many people fleeing the church in droves. Who wants to live among a pile of dry bones?

But as hopeless as our situation might seem, there is always the possibility of resurrection. It will take a miracle, to be sure, but resurrection always does. Resurrection is about new life, and new life is only possible when the breath of God blows through the world. While we may be surrounded by dry bones, we remain godbreathed, in-Spirit-ed people capable of doing miraculous things. We are children of the living God in whom the very breath of creation flows. Not on account of anything

we have done or achieved or earned, but as an act of relentless and never-ending grace from God. These bones can live.
The church can have a future. The Bible can be relevant and
life-giving once more.

But whether or not that fresh wind will blow through this
valley of dry bones is ultimately up to you and me. We are the
godbreathed miracle we are waiting on. We are God's life-giving
act of love to the world. Not because of any special ability of
our own, but because God has chosen to breathe into us the
very breath of creation, the Spirit of life that blows through
every corner of the world and through every person living in
it. If we want to see change, if we want the church to be the
sort of people in and for the world that we were created to be,
if we want the Bible to be a book of life instead of an instru-
ment of death, then it is up to us to breathe the Spirit back
into its pages. It is up to us to be like Ezekiel, to humbly heed
the challenge laid before us by God, and to set the Spirit free
to blow anew through the valley of death we now call home.

As audacious and impossible as that sounds, we can heed
this calling because we are godbreathed people with a godbreathed story to tell. But to tell that story we have to be bold
and willing to love relentlessly and creatively, just as God first
loved us. We have to be willing to love no matter how hard it
might be, love no matter who it might be, and love no matter
what it might cost us. Since we have only one word for love
in English, it can be easy to fall into the trap of thinking that
loving our neighbor means having warm fuzzy feelings inside
our hearts for them. But that isn't godbreathed love. Godbreathed love flows out of us and into the world, transforming
the world into a more welcoming, just, and life-giving place.
Which ironically makes loving our neighbor far more difficult
than fundamentalism. As rigid, legalistic, cruel, and callous as

fundamentalism can be, finding new, creative, life-giving ways to love and serve people we may not want to love and serve can be much more difficult than not drinking beer, not swearing, and not going to see R-rated movies.

That sort of love in action can be a scary thing. But our story reminds us to fear not, for God is by our side. And not just by our side, but in the very air we breathe, animating our imagination with the same creative Spirit that gave birth to all of creation. We need not fear the gatekeepers and naysayers, the demagogues and religious leaders, because the same Spirit that raised Jesus from the dead lives inside of you and me and is just waiting to burst forth and bring a bit of resurrection to every corner of the world. We need not fear the religious leaders who damn us to hell for loving relentlessly, because loving relentlessly is what we were created to do. We were created out of love and loving others is what we are being called into.

Nor do we need to be afraid of failing. We are going to stumble and fall and embarrass ourselves along the way. In our pursuit of being the sort of godbreathed people we are created to be in and for the world, we are going to sometimes fail to love, but so has everyone who has come before us who has tried to do the same. The story of the Bible, the story of the people of God, is the story of people who rarely live up to their calling. Just look at the list of heroes of the faith in Hebrews 11. Not a single one of them was perfect and yet all were commended for their faithfulness, because being imperfect people is okay. Imperfection shouldn't stop us from living out the good news because, as we've seen time and again, the gospel isn't good news because it's perfect. It's good news because it breathes new life into a world of death, and we don't have to be perfect to proclaim that message.

Perfect or not, to love like we are called to love we have to know we are free. For too long we have been shackled by legalism and dogma, the fear of hell, and the shame of never being able to live up to expectations of perfection. But we were created to be free. Free to be curious, free to doubt, free to ask questions, free to hope, free to love, free to disagree, free to deconstruct, and free to dismantle systems of injustice and oppression wherever they may be—including and especially inside the church.

If the story of the Bible is really as good and true and life-giving as we believe it is, then there should be nothing we cannot question or doubt. Good stories stand on their own. Truth can withstand even the most severe inquisition. The Bible teaches us as much. It's a story filled with hard questions about life and death, doubt and forgiveness, fear and loss. And it's a story about a God who is not afraid to listen.

So be fearless in your God-given freedom to ask questions, be curious, and imagine a world where the least are not lost, the sick are not abandoned, the stranger is welcomed, and the poor made rich. Let the breath of the Creator that flows inside you spur you to never-ending curiosity about the world around you and the people in it. Because being godbreathed isn't just about the freedom to ask questions and imagine a better world, but the obligation to do so, to put the gifts we have been given to work for the world around us.

Us.

Even in our freedom we are still bound together as one people with one story and one Spirit. We may feel isolated and alone sometimes. We may literally be isolated and alone sometimes. But our lungs are filled with the same Spirit. That Spirit binds us together as one people so that we are never really alone, even in our darkest moments of despair. She does this most often through the Bible itself. It's part of why it exists. The Bible doesn't just tell stories. In telling our story it brings us together across time and space, culture and context, by serving as a physical reminder that we are not alone in the journey of life.

To be godbreathed is to tell a good and true story. So let us tell a good and true story. And let us tell it honestly, never being afraid to admit our failings, our doubts, our frustrations, our pain, our anger, our hope, and yes, even our ignorance. Let us be humble in our storytelling so that the truth of our story is not found in demagoguery or theatrics or sophisticated rhetoric, but in a life worth living.

Which is why, ultimately, whether or not the bones of the church or the bones of the Bible live and breathe more life into the world comes down to us and what we think the point of being a follower of Jesus is—what it really means to be a godbreathed people entrusted with telling a godbreathed story.

This is what it means to find a meaning in Scripture that is worthy of God. It's not about doing amazing exegesis or impressing people with neat insights into biblical languages. It's about being a Spirit-filled people who use the godbreathed words of Scripture to become the godbreathed people we were created to be in and for the world.

I can't say it enough: you are godbreathed. *You.* The one reading these words right now. God breathed you into existence and wants you to find your story within the story of faith that has already been told and is being told all around you. This is the calling of all godbreathed things, whether that be the written word or flesh and bone—to be godbreathed, to be filled with the Spirit of God, to be filled with love and wonder and share that love and wonder with the rest of the world just as God first shared it with us. We cannot make any claim to believing the Bible is godbreathed if that belief in a godbreathed word doesn't lead us to love our godbreathed neighbors just as God first loved us.

The choice is ours. That's the great beauty and the great risk God takes in breathing out people and trusting them with good news. God trusts us to tell true stories, to live good stories, to love good stories. The question is: Will our story be one that anyone wants to read, let alone live? If it will, it won't be because the story we tell is exciting and miraculous, but because it's full of truth and overflowing with love.

ACKNOWLEDGMENTS

If I'm being completely honest, I find the acknowledgments section the hardest thing to write in a book. Not because I'm ungrateful, but because so many people deserve to be thanked, so many to whose direct and indirect help and insight I am indebted that I will inevitably, but unintentionally, leave someone out who deserves my gratitude.

I can't thank my wife Kim enough for her never-ending love and support. I know that is a cliché, but whatever career I have as a writer would not exist without her for more reasons than I can list. I probably owe my kids more an apology than thanks as they ask me nearly every day "Are you done with your book yet?" so we can play together, but their never-ending patience with me has been a true blessing. I can't say thank you enough to my pastor Shawna and my brother-in-BBQ Kevin for reading a draft of this book so that it might have a chance of being better now than it was when it appeared in their inboxes. Sharing your writing with others can be a terrifying proposition for a writer, but their kindness and eagerness to read it relieved much of that anxiety. Thank you to Amy, Laura, Elisabeth, and all the truly incredible people at Herald Press for once again taking a chance on publishing my work and being so wonderful to work with each and every step of the way. Thank you to my professors. All of them. From undergrad to graduate school, both mentioned in this book and not, you have shaped me in immeasurable ways I can never pay back. And finally, thank you to every single one of you who has ever taken the time to read and support my writing. It is cliché for writers to thank their readers in the acknowledgments of their books, but I mean those thanks sincerely and from the bottom of my heart. This book quite literally would not exist without you.

NOTES

CHAPTER 1

1. I was once a youth pastor and can now admit we are not as funny as we lead ourselves to believe.
2. The books of the prophets are in large part a direct response to the idolatry and injustice practiced by Israel. Major prophets like Isaiah, Jeremiah, and Ezekiel, minor prophets like Malachi and Hosea, and even the Psalms all warn about the dangers of idolatry because Israel is worshiping other gods alongside or in place of Yahweh.
3. John J. Collins, *Introduction to the Hebrew Bible* (Minneapolis: Fortress Press, 2018), 632.

CHAPTER 2

1. An easy to read but nevertheless exhaustive history of how the Bible came together can be found in John Barton, *A History of the Bible: The Book and Its Faiths* (London: Penguin Random House UK, 2020).
2. Barton, 23.
3. Barton, 32.
4. Barton, 113.
5. Barton, 28.
6. Barton, 31.
7. Barton, 85.
8. Barton, 238.
9. Barton, 164.
10. Bart D. Ehrman, *The Orthodox Corruption of Scripture: The Effect of Early Christological Controversies on the Text of the New Testament* (New York: Oxford University Press, 2011), 26.
11. Barton, *A History of the Bible*, 160.
12. Harry Y. Gamble, *The New Testament Canon: Its Making and Meaning* (Eugene, OR: Wipf and Stock Publishers, 1985), 24.

13. See Matthew D. C. Larsen, *Gospels before the Book* (New York: Oxford University Press, 2018) as well as John Barton, *How the Bible Came to Be* (Louisville, KY: Westminster John Knox, 1998).
14. Gamble, *New Testament Canon*, 24.
15. Barton, *A History of the Bible*, 200.
16. Barton, 203–5.
17. Ehrman, *Orthodox Corruption*, 22.
18. Barton, *A History of the Bible*, 266
19. Barton, 246.
20. Barton, 265.
21. Bruce M. Metzger, *The Canon of the New Testament: Its Origin, Development, and Significance* (New York: Oxford University Press, 1997), 304–315.
22. Metzger, *Canon of the New Testament*, 271.
23. Ehrman, *Orthodox Corruption*, 7–9.
24. Barton, *A History of the Bible*, 354.
25. *Nova*, season 47, episode 13, "A to Z: The First Alphabet," directed by David Sington, aired September 20, 2020, on PBS, https://www.pbs.org/wgbh/nova/video/a-to-z-the-first-alphabet/.
26. Barton, *A History of the Bible*, 358.
27. Barton, 358.
28. Barton, 37.
29. Barton, 37.
30. Ehrman, *Orthodox Corruption*, 31.
31. Ehrman, 31.
32. Barton, *A History of the Bible*, 362.
33. Barton, 362.
34. Barton, 10.
35. For a good overview of this development see chapter two of Brad S. Gregory's *The Unintended Reformation: How a Religious Revolution Secularized Society* (Cambridge, MA: Belknap Press, 2015).
36. Barton, *A History of the Bible*, 467.

CHAPTER 3

1. See Augustine's treatise *The Literal Meaning of Genesis*.
2. George M. Marsden, *Fundamentalism and American Culture* (New York: Oxford University Press, 2006), 20.
3. Jeffrey Tigay, "Genesis as Allegory: Recognizing the Deeper Meaning of the Text," *My Jewish Learning*, https://www.myjewishlearning.com/article/genesis-as-allegory/.
4. John MacArthur, ed., *The Inerrant Word: Biblical, Historical, Theological, and Pastoral Perspectives* (Wheaton, IL: Crossway, 2016), 117.

5. "How Have Christians Responded to Darwin's 'Origin of Species'?," BioLogos.org, https://biologos.org/common-questions/how-have-christians-responded-to-darwins-origin-of-species.

6. Marsden, *Fundamentalism*, 119.

7. Marsden, 118–23.

8. "Minutes of the General Assembly of the Presbyterian Church in the United States of America," 1910, https://archive.org/details/minutesofgeneral1910pres/page/n7/mode/2up?view=theater.

9. Marsden, *Fundamentalism*, 167.

10. Marsden, 169–70.

11. Henry Emerson Fosdick, "Shall the Fundamentalists Win?," June 10, 1922, http://historymatters.gmu.edu/d/5070/.

12. Marsden, *Fundamentalism*, 185.

13. Marsden, 192.

14. Marsden, 185.

15. For a comprehensive look at how American fundamentalism rose, fell, and rose again see Marsden, *Fundamentalism and American Culture*.

16. MacArthur, *Inerrant Word*, 175–76, 374.

17. Norman L. Geisler and William C. Roach, eds., *Defending Inerrancy: Affirming the Accuracy of Scripture for a New Generation* (Grand Rapids, MI: Baker Books, 2011), 20.

18. Geisler and Roach, *Defending*, 22–23.

19. *NPR*, "Southern Baptists Apologize for Slavery Stance," August 28, 2009, https://www.npr.org/templates/story/story.php?storyId=112329862.

20. Geisler and Roach, *Defending*, 35.

21. MacArthur, *Inerrant Word*, 117.

22. MacArthur, 124.

23. MacArthur, 118.

24. MacArthur, 116.

25. *Westminster Confession*, Chapter 1, https://www.pcaac.org/wp-content/uploads/2022/04/WCFScripureProofs2022.pdf.

26. *Westminster Confession*, Chapter 1.

27. *Westminster Confession*, Chapter 1.

28. *Westminster Confession*, Chapter 1.

29. *Westminster Confession*, Chapter 1.

30. Brad S. Gregory, *The Unintended Reformation: How a Religious Revolution Secularized Society* (Cambridge, MA: Belknap Press, 2015), 100–101.

CHAPTER 4

1. I use "he" because until we recently elected our first female pastor, every preceding pastor in our church's history had been male.

2. I grew up in the Church of the Nazarene. Although originally named the Pentecostal Church of the Nazarene, Pentecostal was dropped after the denomination was founded to distinguish the Church of the Nazarene from churches in the charismatic tradition.

3. For more on this idea see my book *Unraptured: How End Times Theology Gets It Wrong* (Harrisonburg, VA: Herald Press, 2019).

4. Clinton E. Arnold, "Who Wrote Ephesians?," Zondervan Academic, December 11, 2019, https://zondervanacademic.com/blog/who-wrote-ephesians.

5. John J. Collins, *Introduction to the Hebrew Bible* (Minneapolis: Fortress Press, 2018), 53–63.

6. Collins, *Introduction*.

7. It was me.

8. John Barton, *How the Bible Came to Be* (Louisville, KY: Westminster John Knox, 1998), 189.

9. Bart D. Ehrman, *The Orthodox Corruption of Scripture: The Effect of Early Christological Controversies on the Text of the New Testament* (New York: Oxford University Press, 2011), 31.

10. Matthew D. C. Larsen, *Gospels before the Book* (New York: Oxford University Press, 2018), 4.

11. John MacArthur, ed., *The Inerrant Word: Biblical, Historical, Theological, and Pastoral Perspectives* (Wheaton, IL: Crossway, 2016), 210–30.

12. R. Allen Culpepper, "Luke," *The New Interpreter's Bible: A Commentary in Twelve Volumes*, 9:62.

13. Culpepper, 62.

14. Daniel J. Harrington, *The Gospel of Matthew*, Sacra Pagina, vol. 1 (Collegeville, MN: Liturgical Press, 1991), 47.

15. Collins, *Introduction*, 108.

16. Collins, 197.

17. Collins, 197.

18. Biblical Archeology Society, "The Tel Dan Inscription: The First Historical Evidence of King David from the Bible," June 14, 2022, https://www.biblicalarchaeology.org/daily/biblical-artifacts/the-tel-dan-inscription-the-first-historical-evidence-of-the-king-david-bible-story/.

19. MacArthur, *Inerrant Word*, 244–54.

20. MacArthur, 17.

21. MacArthur, 134–46.

22. Martin Luther, *Word and Sacrament*, Luther's Works, vol. 35 (Fortress Press, 1960), 362.

23. Augustine, *Literal Commentary on Genesis*, Library of Congress, https://tile.loc.gov/storage-services/service/gdc/gdcwdl/wd/l_/14/70/6/wdl_14706/wdl_14706.pdf.

24. Origen, *On First Principles* (Notre Dame, IN: Christian Classics, 2013), 378.

CHAPTER 5

1. Made you look.
2. I hate potlucks almost as much as I hate casseroles.
3. Rachel Held Evans, "Everyone's a Biblical Literalist Until You Bring Up Gluttony," July 8, 2013, https://rachelheldevans.com/blog/literalist-gluttony.
4. For more on Revelation see my book *Unraptured: How End Times Theology Gets It Wrong* (Harrisonburg, VA: Herald Press, 2019).
5. Origen, *On First Principles* (Notre Dame, IN: Christian Classics, 2013), 381.

CHAPTER 6

1. John MacArthur, ed., *The Inerrant Word: Biblical, Historical, Theological, and Pastoral Perspectives* (Wheaton, IL: Crossway, 2016), 17.
2. Tom Gjelten, "Southern Baptist Seminary Confronts History of Slaveholding and 'Deep Racism,'" *NPR*, December 13, 2018, https://www.npr.org/2018/12/13/676333342/southern-baptist-seminary-confronts-history-of-slaveholding-and-deep-racism.
3. Joseph W. Trigg, *Origen* (New York: Routledge, 1998), 15.
4. Henri Croulez, *Origen: The Life and Thought of the First Great Theologian* (Worcester, UK: Harper & Row, 1989), xii.
5. Croulez, 9.
6. Origen, De Principiis (Book IV), New Advent, https://www.newadvent.org/fathers/04124.htm.
7. Origen, 378–81.
8. Origen, 374.

CHAPTER 7

1. #Humblebrag.
2. Chris Bounds, "The Wesleyan Quadrilateral," *The Wesleyan Church*, January 24, 2022, https://www.wesleyan.org/the-wesleyan-quadrilateral.
3. See Miguel A. De La Torre, *Decolonizing Christianity: Becoming Badass Believers*; Richard Twist, *Rescuing the Gospel from the Cowboys: A Native American Expression of the Jesus Way*; Will Gafney, *Womanist Midrash: A Reintroduction to the Women of the Torah and the Throne*; Hugh R. Page Jr., ed., *The Africana Bible: Reading Israel's Scriptures from Africa and the African Diaspora*; and Pablo Richard, *Apocalypse: A People's Commentary on the Book of Revelation*; among many others.
4. Augustine, *On Christian Teaching* (New York: Oxford University Press, 2008), 27.

5. Augustine, 9.

6. See Keegan Osinski, *Queering Wesley, Queering the Church*; Matthew Vines, *God and the Gay Christian*; Justin Lee, *Torn: Rescuing the Gospel from the Gays-vs.-Christians Debate*; and Mihee Kim-Kort, *Outside the Lines: How Embracing Queerness Will Transform Your Faith*; among others.

CHAPTER 8

1. Katheryn Pfisterer Darr, "The Book of Ezekiel," *The New Interpreter's Bible: A Commentary in Twelve Volumes* (Nashville: Abingdon Press, 1994), 5:1500.

2. Pew Research Center, "Modeling the Future of Religion in America," September 13, 2022, https://www.pewresearch.org/religion/2022/09/13/projecting-u-s-religious-groups-population-shares-by-2070/.

3. Pew Research Center, "In U.S., Decline of Christianity Continues at Rapid Pace," October 17, 2019, https://www.pewresearch.org/religion/2019/10/17/in-u-s-decline-of-christianity-continues-at-rapid-pace/.

THE AUTHOR

Zack Hunt has been writing about the interplay of faith and politics in the public sphere for the last decade, both on his eponymous blog and Patheos, as well as contributing articles to multiple publications including *The Huffington Post, Relevant Magazine, Ministry Matters, Youth Worker Journal,* and many more. These years of writing culminated in the successful launch of his first book, *Unraptured.* A graduate of Trevecca Nazarene University, he also holds a graduate degree in theology as well as an additional graduate degree in Christian history from Yale Divinity School. Combined with more than twenty years spent preaching and working in various forms of ministry, Zack is perfectly positioned to continue his work reimagining the church's relationship with the Bible and its role in the lives of believers. When not writing about the intersection of faith and politics, Zack can be found traveling and trying out new restaurants with his wife, playing with their two little girls, and sneaking out onto his back porch trying to smoke the perfect rack of ribs on his beloved smoker.